This is the best
and most helpful book
on commodities ever written

It gives you the rules
and methods professionals use

How To
Build A Fortune
in
COMMODITIES

by
R. C. ALLEN

REVISED EDITION

WINDSOR BOOKS

Box 280, Brightwaters, N.Y. 11718

Other books by

R. C. ALLEN

The Secret of Success

How To Build A Fortune and Save On Taxes

The Truth About Life Insurance

William Penn Patrick

The World's Best Bits Of Wisdom

Professional Trading System

Published by Windsor Books
P.O. Box 280
Brightwaters, N.Y. 11718

Manufactured in the United States of America
ISBN 0-930233-12-3

Caveat: It should be noted that all commodity trades, patterns, charts, systems, etc., discussed in this book are for illustrative purposes only and are not to be construed as specific advisory recommendations. Further note that no method of trading or investing is foolproof or without difficulty, and past performance is no guarantee of future performance. All ideas and material presented are entirely those of the author and do not necessarily reflect those of the publisher or bookseller.

TABLE OF CONTENTS

R. C. ALLEN

The author of this book, R. C. Allen, has been associated with commodity trading for more than thirty years. And he has developed good relationships with hundreds of brokers and professional traders in every area of the United States, Canada and London, England.

He was President of International Commodity Advisors, Inc., advisor and consultant to the "Special Situations Commodity Service." He is also the originator of the 4 day, 9 day and 18 day moving averages. This commodity trend indicator, together with his "Precision Timing Tool," helps to make his advice more profitable than the advice of others who do not use these tools.

In 1955, Mr. Allen was the first man to point out, on a nationwide basis, why life insurance stocks offer an unusual opportunity for large capital gains. His interesting, fact-filled book, *"How To Build A Fortune And Save On Taxes"* opened the eyes of several million people to the unusual potential for profit in life insurance stocks at that time.

The above book, together with *"The Truth About Life Insurance"* and the special reports on life insurance policies written by Mr. Allen, helped to motivate investment-minded people to start more than six hundred new life insurance companies. Sales in those companies now total several billions of dollars in life insurance and their assets have helped to expand the economy of the United States.

R. C. Allen is also the author of *"The Secret Of Success"*. This international best-seller is a living classic. It is one of those rare books that thousands of people buy in quantity to give to their friends and business associates.

R. C. Allen believes that commodity trading is now entering its second phase of growth. With this book, a larger number of traders can learn how to overcome some of the mistakes that are, so often, made. When this is done, they will then be able to earn larger profits.

It is hoped, therefore, that this valuable book will serve as a reference and a guide for those millions of people who would like to know *How to Build A Fortune In Commodities.*

Windsor Books

1

A FASCINATING WAY TO EARN MORE MONEY

This book was written to help millions of investment-minded men and women find an answer to three basic facts:

1. You can't get rich by working. You have to put some money to work and let your money work for you.

2. To earn a larger amount of money, you must have knowledge, know-how, capital and courage.

3. The more you know, the more you understand and the more careful you are to seek out the best opportunities, the greater your success can be.

With that in mind, you might be interested to know that only 1 man in 1,000 knows *how to build a fortune in commodities*—but it can be done. If you are on the right side of a fast-moving market, the amount of money you can earn is tremendous.

For example—a 6 cent move in Live Cattle can result in a profit of $2,360. That is a profit of 118% on a margin of $2,000. And that 6 cent move may occur as often as two to three times every year.

A 30 cent move in Corn can result in a profit of $1,470. That is 98% on a margin of $1,500. A 10 cent move in Cocoa can result in a profit of 147% on a margin of $2,000. A 10 cent move in Pork Bellies (uncured bacon) can result in a profit of $3,720 per contract. That is a profit of $2,220 on a margin of $1,500. A 50 cent move in Wheat can result in a profit of 50% on a margin of $1,000. And a 40 cent move in Silver can result in a profit of $3,920—131% on a margin of $3,000.

While those profits are realistic and possible, you can have a loss if you are wrong. But, if you will follow the rules, ideas and plans contained in this book, the profits you earn can always be larger than your losses.

In brief, commodity trading, like any good profession, is a hard way to make an easy living. Once you learn how to trade and understand what to do, you can earn a profit of 30% per month—360% or more—every year for as long as you live.

All you need to do is follow the rules and plans contained in this book. Read and re-read each one and study them carefully because each rule and plan was developed after 30 years of trading, making mistakes, learning from those mistakes and putting those rules and plans to work.

Now you can benefit from that knowledge and, hopefully, you will never make as many mistakes as I have made. Once you learn the rules and know *what to do* and *what not to do*, you will then find it easier to *build a fortune in commodities.*

WHAT IS A FORTUNE?

Webster's Dictionary says, "Fortune is — success, good luck, prosperity."

If you look at the word "fortune" in that light and do not try to "get rich overnight" or insist you want to become a millionaire between now and next year, you can successfully trade in commodities and earn from $7,000 to $100,000 every year — either full time or part time — depending on how much money you have in your commodity account.

I use the figure of $100,000 as a maximum per year because, after talking with hundreds of traders over the past thirty years — both amateur and professional — I sincerely believe it is psychologically difficult for anyone, including the professional, to earn more than $100,000 *every year* while trading in commodities. So with that in mind, any "fortune" you hope to make should have a conservative goal of $100,000 per year.

Only a genius could do better—and that type of mind is very rare. If you have that type of mind then you might earn more than $100,000 per year.

Once you know how, you can earn that large amount of money every year while devoting only a few hours each day and a few days each week. Commodity trading, therefore, can be a very profitable activity. It is also an ideal activity for an individual who has retired and wants to occupy his or her mind with an interesting pastime for a few hours each day.

Obviously, if you should earn $100,000 per year, you could invest a large part of your earnings in high-grade bonds, carefully selected stocks or good real estate. If you have good luck in your choices, they could help you to become considerably more wealthy over a period of years.

Yes, you can *build a fortune* if you try. But, to do so, I suggest you —

1. **Read and re-read this book carefully —at least three times.**

2. **Underline or circle the key points you should never forget.**

3. **Trade lightly at first until you gain a certain feel, know-how and understanding of each market.**

A great many books and courses have been written on commodity trading. I have read and studied them all. After you boil them down, take out the unnecessary words and eliminate many of the confusing viewpoints, you will find that the ideas, rules and principles contained in this book are the ones that will help you the most if you sincerely want to earn some money from trading in commodities.

Realistically, you should be conservative. Try to earn no more than an average of 30% per month (360% per year). This means that, if your investment in commodities is $3,000, you can earn $10,800 per year. If your investment is $5,000, you can earn $18,000. With $10,000, you can earn $36,000. And, with $30,000 you may be able to earn $100,000.

Some readers may say, "If it is possible to earn $36,000 on an investment of $10,000, why isn't it possible to trade with $100,000 and earn $360,000?"

The reason is — if you try to earn more than $100,000 per year, you may eventually lose because the human mind is not able to be continually right—or lucky—all of the time. In fact, very few traders can consistently, year after year, earn more than $100,000 in commodities. It requires too much study, concentration, and constant control over your emotions.

You must also follow all of the rules in Chapter 10. This, in brief, is the answer to *HOW TO BUILD A FORTUNE IN COMMODITIES.*

With a maximum goal of $100,000 in mind, you can now settle down, plan your strategy and make a sincere effort to earn that 30% average per month. But, to do it, you will need to read this book over and over — especially Chapter 10 — until your understanding becomes quite clear. You will then begin to think like a professional and your success will be more certain.

WHAT IS A PROFESSIONAL?

A professional is one who has trained himself in a field where the majority of others in that field are considered amateurs. This is true of the legal profession, medicine, engineering, music and sports.

Professional ballplayers, golfers, boxers, and musicians spend many hours each day for many months polishing their skills until they feel ready to meet their competition. If professional athletes know it is wise to do this — why don't amateurs do it?

Unfortunately, amateurs who try to compete with professionals are unable to do so for very long because they fail to put in the large amount of time and effort necessary to perfect their ability.

The reason is — amateurs are mentally lazy. They will never earn the same amount of money as professionals because — *they are satisfied, too easily, with mediocrity.*

Somehow they feel they are as good as the professionals. Even when they lose, they try to justify themselves. They cannot believe it happened to them.

Professionals however, don't like to make mistakes. In the majority of cases, they will win because they know the right moves to make—at the right time.

Sometimes, they lose but they study, learn, correct whatever mistakes they make—then try to do better the next time.

Some tips from professional traders are given in Chapter 18. Get their view point. You will then have a better understanding of this necessary and important business of commodities.

COMMODITIES —
THE WORLD'S LARGEST BUSINESS

Commodity trading is the world's largest business. And each year, it grows larger. In 1945, only 200,000 individuals and companies traded in commodities. In 1982, the number had grown to 600,000. By 1990, there may be 1,000,000 or more.

Another fact is — the gross value of contracts traded in the 20 most active commodities is larger than the total dollar volume of trading done in the shares of the more than 1,800 large companies listed on the New York Stock Exchange.

In 1974, the total dollar volume of trading on the various Commodity Exchanges totaled more than $300 billion. This is more than double the $133 billion total dollar volume of the New York Stock Exchange.

As millions of people become better informed about this important and necessary business, several million investors in Wall St. stocks will switch some of their funds from the slow-moving and sometimes boring stocks to the faster-moving and more exciting commodities.

That is why the total volume of commodity trading should continue to grow and, by 1990, the total volume of trading may exceed $600 billion—more than triple the amount of trading that is expected for stocks.

Obviously, there must be a reason for this growing interest in commodities.

COMMODITIES ARE INTERESTING AND EXCITING

Commodity trading is one of the most interesting activities you can engage in. Something is always happening — or — going to happen. And, best of all, the profits you can earn in commodities are larger, percentagewise, than the profits in any other business — if you are right in your judgment.

Furthermore, commodity trading is more exciting than stocks and bonds. It is also more important. Why? Because you can do without stocks and bonds, but

no one anywhere in the world can do without one or more commodities for even one day.

Commodities are the basic necessities of life. They consist of what you eat, what you wear and whatever you need to build a house, run a store or operate any form of business or trade.

The 20 most popular commodities for "speculators" in 1982 were—

Live Cattle	Silver
Corn	Sugar
Soybeans	Copper
Soybean Oil	T Bills
Wheat	Plywood
Live Hogs	Foreign Currencies
Pork Bellies	S & P Index
Cocoa	Lumber
Cotton	Oats
Soybean Meal	Frozen Orange Juice

All of the above commodities are traded through a "futures contract." A futures contract is an agreement to buy or sell a specified amount of a commodity at an agreed upon price for delivery during a specified month — in the future.

12 GOOD REASONS
FOR TRADING IN COMMODITIES

After you read this book and understand the importance of commodities, you will realize that trading in these necessities is oftentimes easier, safer and more interesting than trading in stocks, bonds or real estate.

In contrast to the New York Stock Exchange, which many informed people call, "A very private club operated strictly for the benefit of its members," commodity trading has 12 definite advantages. When millions of people understand these advantages, there will be a tremendous increase in commodity trading.

1. It is the only business I know of in which a man with reasonable intelligence, an investment of only a few thousand dollars and a careful, conservative approach to earning money has the same chance to *build a fortune* in an important business activity as the man with many years of training and experience.

2. No equity in the world is as liquid nor sold as easily as one of the 20 important commodities traded on the major commodity exchanges.

   A position can usually be bought or sold within one or two minutes. You do not have to search for a buyer or a seller, wait for an auction or undergo days and weeks of discussion. And there are no loans to arrange nor days and weeks of frustration waiting to close a sale as is the case when you deal in real estate.

3. Nowhere I know of can you get every dollar you are entitled to as fast as from a broker who trades in commodities. It never takes more than one day and, in an emergency, most brokers will give you a check the same day — if your account is in proper balance.

4. The amount of money due you is guaranteed. If your broker also deals in stocks, he could go broke (as many stock brokerage firms, large and small, have done in the past). In such a case, you may have to wait many months or years to get all or part of your money. But each Commodity Exchange requires that money used by brokers for commodity accounts must be kept separate from the securities accounts. Reputable brokers, therefore, keep your commodity money intact so you can always get that money when you need it.

5. Smaller margins are required. Usually only 5% to 10% of the total amount of the contract. This gives you a leverage on your money 10 to 20 times larger than the same amount of money invested in stocks. As a result, every $3,000 you invest in commodities can earn you as much money as $30,000 to $60,000 invested in stocks.

6. There are no "insiders" or "dealers behind the scenes" similar to those in the stock market. In the commodity markets, all of the important facts and information are made available to all those who are interested — at the same time. And traders may act or not act upon that information as they choose.

   No favoritism is shown. The U.S. Government Commodity Exchange Authority works to prevent fraud, manipulation and the spreading of false rumors. Their constant surveillance makes it impossible for any large speculator to "corner the market."

   Any major news that might drastically affect prices in any commodity is released to the public only after a market has closed. This allows everyone interested in that information to analyze the statistics and prepare to buy or sell according to his own judgment when the market opens the next day.

7. It costs less to trade in commodities than in stocks, bonds or real estate. The commissions are lower. For example, the commission on one contract of Wheat with a value of $17,500 (5,000 bushels at $3.50 per bushel) is only $70. That is less than one-half of 1% of the total value of the contract and is the only commission you pay for the entire transaction—both purchase and sale.

   In stocks, on a purchase of $17,500, you would pay a commission of $156 plus another $156 when you sell those shares. The total commission for both the purchase and sale of those shares is $312. That is more than 4 times the total commission for both the purchase and sale of Wheat, Corn or Soybeans.

   In Pork Bellies, the commission of one contract of 38,000 pounds with a value of $26,600 (38,000 pounds at 70 cents per pound) is $75. The commission on both the purchase and sale of $26,000 of stocks is $825—11 times more than the $75 commission for Pork Bellies.

8. You have an excellent tax advantage. Long-term capital gains in commodities can help you save on taxes just as they do in stocks, bonds and real estate.

9. You have the opportunity to earn an extra amount of money—without putting up any more money. When you hold a long position in a certain commodity and you feel that a temporary decline in price may occur, you can sell the same quantity of that commodity "short" in a different option month and try to take advantage of that possible decline in price. Or, if you are "short" and you believe that prices may move up, you can buy a similar amount in a different option month (without putting up additional money) in an effort to gain a profit from a temporary rise in prices.

   You cannot do that in the stock market unless you put up additional money and "sell against the box" or put up some money for a "put" or a "call."

10. It is easy to sell short in commodities if you believe that prices may go lower. When you trade in stocks, a short sale can be made only on an "up tick" in the market for that stock. But, in commodities, that up-tick is not necessary. If you want to sell short, your order to sell will be executed immediately. This saves you much time and frustration.

11. The news, facts and information you need to know are readily available. None is hidden. This is in direct contrast to the stock market where the news and information concerning a company may be kept secret for several weeks or months until the "insiders" have had a chance to buy or sell.

     You will also find it is easier to read and consider news on only 20 major commodities than it is to read and digest the information given out on 30,000 stocks, thousands of bonds and hundreds of mutual funds that compete with one another on the stock exchanges.

12. Finally, commodity trading is simple. You need not be concerned with stock certificates, proxies, voting rights, ex-dividend dates, conversions, mergers, "spin-offs" and other corporate matters that often confuse those who trade in stocks and bonds.

SMALLER MARGINS GIVE YOU MORE LEVERAGE

The individuals who earn the largest amount of money understand the importance of "leverage" and how to use it. In commodities, the margin required is small—usually only 5% to 10% of the total value of the contract. This gives you a high rate of "leverage." You can, therefore, start with a smaller amount of capital and, with careful, conservative trading, you can *build a fortune* in a shorter period of time.

With only 5% to 10% margin, every dollar you invest has the ability to multiply your profits 10 to 20 times faster than would be possible if you put up the 100% margin that may be required when you buy stocks.

The following figures illustrate the average margin required for each contract. The total value of each contract may vary as the price goes up or down. But, as a general rule, the margin will seldom change—except in cases where prices have risen rapidly to a high level and the total value of each contract has increased substantially.

At those high levels, prices may swing wildly up and down for several weeks. The increase in the margin will then reflect that increase in the value of the contract. It will also help to calm down the over-optimistic market. Later, as prices decline to more reasonable levels, the margin will be reduced.

Commodity	Price	Size of Contract	Total Value	Margin	Per Cent
Broilers - Iced	.32	28,000 lbs.	$8,960	$600	6.7%
Cattle - Live	.40	40,000 lbs.	$16,000	$1,500	9.4%
Cocoa	.40	30,000 lbs.	$12,000	$1,500	12.5%
Copper	.60	25,000 lbs.	$15,000	$1,500	10%
Corn	2.00	5,000 bus.	$10,000	$1,000	15%
Cotton	.36	50,000 lbs.	$18,000	$1,000	5.6%
Eggs - Shell	.35	21,000 doz.	$7,350	$500	6.8%
Hogs - Live	.35	30,000 lbs.	$10,500	$1,000	10%
Lumber	$100.	90,000 ft.	$9,000	$500	5.6%
Oats	.95	10,000 bus.	$9,500	$800	8.5%
Orange Juice	.50	15,000 lbs.	$7,500	$750	10%
Plywood	100.	69,120 sq. ft.	$6,912	$500	7.2%
Pork Bellies	.40	36,000 lbs.	$14,400	$1,200	8.4%
Potatoes	.05	50,000 lbs.	$2,500	$400	16%
Silver	$2.00	10,000 ozs.	$20,000	$1,500	7.5%
Soybeans	$5.00	5,000 bus.	$25,000	$2,500	10%
Soybean Meal	$90 ton	20,000 lbs.	$9,000	$800	8.9%
Soybean Oil	.15	60,000 lbs.	$9,000	$800	8.9%
Sugar	.08	112,000 lbs.	$8,960	$1,200	14%
Wheat	$2.50	5,000 bus.	$12,500	$1,000	8%

The 20 examples above show you why, with such a small margin, it is possible to gain a profit of 30% to 100% or more in only a few weeks. And, of course, if you are wrong in your judgment, you can also lose that amount in the same period of time. It is important, therefore, to follow the rules in Chapter 10 of this book.

In brief, those rules emphasize the fact you must trade in a careful, conservative manner or you will find it difficult to earn money on a consistent basis.

Greed has always caused commodity traders to, eventually, become losers instead of winners. So be practical. Learn the rules in Chapter 10. Then you will be a winner instead of a loser.

After you decide to trade and your order has been confirmed, you must maintain the amount of margin required by each Commodity Exchange. If you do not keep your margin at the required amount, your broker has the right to close out your contract. Your trade, therefore, will show a loss.

LARGE PROFITS ARE POSSIBLE

With a leverage of 10 to 20 in your favor, it does not take much capital to build a fortune in commodities. You can start with an amount from $3,000 to $10,000.

If you have less than that amount, you may find it wise to start a Commodity Trading Club. (See Chapter 14.) With know-how and understanding, you can increase that capital until, after a few years, you could earn $100,000 per year.

That amount of profit is possible because, with the small margins that are required, a small price change in your favor can give you a tremendous return on your investment.

For example—if you buy 2 contracts of Pork Bellies (uncured bacon) at 60 cents per pound, you will own the rights to 76,000 pounds of bellies with a value of $45,600. The margin required for two contracts is $3,000—approximately 7%. If the market moves up only 6 cents (600 points), your 76,000 pounds of bellies are now worth $50,160 (76,000 x 66 cents). This gives you a net gain of $4,560. That is a profit of 152% on the $3,000 required for margin.

A move of 6 cents occurs many times every year and that 6 cent move with its 152% profit should be your minimum objective. (See Chart 1. Several 96 cent moves are circled).

The big profits in Pork Bellies, however, as in all commodities, will come from the major moves of 6 cents or more. On a move of 6 cents, your profit is $2,210—152% net per contract. (The 6 cent moves are set in a rectangle on that same Pork Belly chart).

If you are fortunate in gaining a profit of 6 cents from either a bull move or a bear move, 152% profit on a single trade is almost one-half of your goal of 360% per year mentioned earlier in this chapter.

Occasionally, Pork Bellies will offer you an opportunity to earn more than 6 cents on either a bull move or a bear move. But, don't count on it. As a "speculator" interested in profits, it is wiser to take a good profit out of the middle. Don't try to get it all. The reason is — many factors will upset your ability to trade conservatively when you try to hold on too long, or try to get the maximum amount of profit.

After you take your profit, stay out of that commodity for

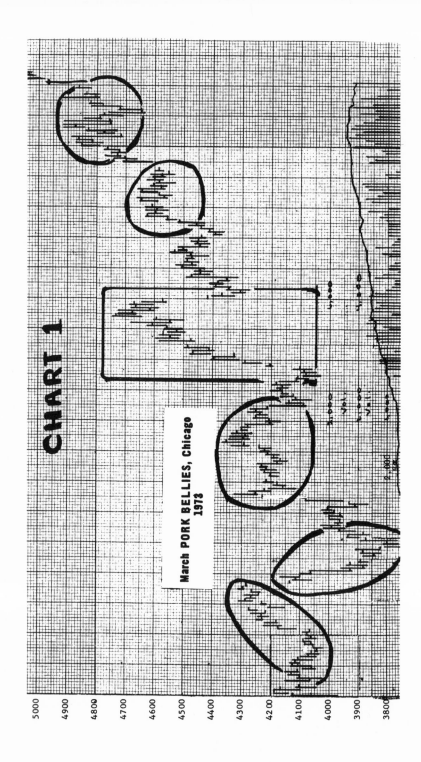

CHART 1

March PORK BELLIES, Chicago
1973

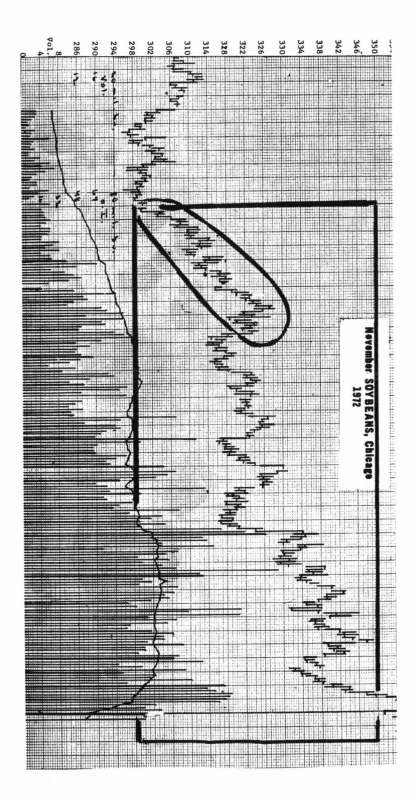

November SOYBEANS, Chicago
1972

a few weeks or more. Look for "special situations" (see Chapter 9) and your fortune may increase.

Let us take another example. Assume you buy 2 contracts of Soybeans. You would then own the rights to 10,000 bushels. At a price of $5.00 per bushel, that would give you a total value of $50,000. The margin required is $6,000— approximately 12%. A move of 50¢ in your favor would give you a profit of $5,000 on those two contracts less $80 commission for a net gain of $4,920—82%. (See Chart 2. Several large moves in Soybeans are circled.)

If Soybeans move $1.00 in your favor, your two contracts would then be worth $60,000. Your profit would be $9,920. On a margin of $6,000 your net gain would be 165%. As in Pork Bellies, it is obviously wise to try to gain as much as you can from the large moves that occur several times each year.

When you learn how to select "special situations" (see chapter 9) and improve your timing, you will find it easier to gain from those big moves.

WHO TRADES IN COMMODITIES?

There are two basic groups who trade in the 20 major commodities. First, there are the "hedgers." They are the commercial interests. The farmers, producers, processors, manufacturers and exporters of those commodities. All of those commercial interests have a large investment in plant and equipment.

They do not speculate. Their main interest is to earn a reasonable profit on the money they have invested in their business. They try, therefore, to "hedge" their inventory, eliminate the speculative risk and protect their business against the possibility of a large loss.

For a better understanding of "hedging," read Chapter 3, "The Importance of Hedging."

Many large corporations trade in commodities every day. They have to do this in order to stay in business. For example, General Mills, Kellogg's and Quaker Oats continually take positions in Wheat, Corn and Oats. Central Soya deals heavily in Soybeans. Corn Products Company deals heavily in Corn. Eastman Kodak and Polaroid deal heavily in Silver for their photographic film. Hershey, Nestle's and others deal heavily in Cocoa. Swift, Armour, Hormel and

Rath deal heavily in Live Hogs and Pork Bellies. Burlington Mills, Cannon and other cotton goods manufacturers deal heavily in Cotton. Weyerhauser and Georgia-Pacific deal heavily in Plywood.

In addition, thousands of banks and lending agencies have a strong interest in commodities. They recommend that all the farmers, processors, manufacturers and exporters who come to them for loans should protect their profits with "hedges" in the futures markets.

The second group of traders are the "speculators." They seldom "hedge.' They know that the high rate of leverage in commodities gives them a tremendous opportunity for a large profit—if they buy the right commodity at the right time. And they are willing to assume the risk involved in an effort to earn that large profit.

A speculator holds a contract for a specified amount of a commodity. In this way, the contract he holds is somewhat similar to a stock certificate. Both stocks and commodities, therefore, are treated as capital assets. Trades in either one will result in either long-term or short-term gains or losses—depending on how long you hold the contract.

Many people confuse speculating with gambling. Few understand the difference. Gambling is basically "guessing". Gamblers, therefore, "hope" they will be "lucky". The professional speculator, however, calculates every move and bases his judgment on information he believes is reliable.

This point becomes more clear when you consider the statement made by Sir Ernest Cossell, private banker to King Edward VI of England.

> When I was young, unknown and started to be successful, I was called a gambler. My operations increased in scope and volume. Then I was known as a speculator. My activities continued to expand. Presently, I am known as a banker. Actually, I had been doing the same thing all the time.

Everyone, everywhere speculates every day. From the time you get out of bed in the morning until you climb back in, you speculate on everything you do.

All life is a speculation. You take a chance when you apply for your first job. You take a chance when you cross the street. You take a chance when you board an airplane. All because you want to accomplish something or reach a certain goal. You believe the odds are in your favor because you gave some thought to how and why you should start.

If you have a job, you go to work each day and speculate that they will keep you on that job. If you own a business, you speculate that someone will buy from you. You extend credit because you speculate that the one who receives that credit will, someday, pay you what he owes. You borrow money because you speculate you will be able to pay it back.

You drive a car and you speculate that none of the thousands of other cars will hit you. You go to a movie and speculate that it will be good. You buy a new suit and speculate it will last a full year. You speculate that you will live another ten, twenty or thirty years. And, if you lose your job or your business, you speculate that you will find another.

The speculations you undergo every year cover a thousand situations. You may make some mistakes and, later, you find you need to change your mind. But you also find that many of the things you did were right. If they were, then at the end of each year, you wind up just a little better off than when the year began.

The same approach should be used in commodities. When you believe the potential for profit is greater than the possible loss, make a trade, watch it carefully and take your profits before they fade away.

TWO KINDS OF SPECULATORS

There are two kinds of speculators. First, are the "scalpers." They are called "locals" or "floor traders" whose place of business is on the trading floor of each Commodity Exchange. Their minute by minute buy and sell orders help to make an orderly and more fluid market.

When the "scalper" trades, he hopes for a small profit—usually 1/8 or 1/4 of a cent in grains and only 5 to 20 points in other commodities.

At the first sign of a loss, the "scalper" will get out of his position before the loss grows larger. And he will seldom carry his position overnight—unless he feels the trend of the market may cause prices to open the next day in his favor.

The second group of speculators are the business and professional men, farmers and other individuals who take a position at a certain price and hold it for several days or months.

The Chicago Mercantile Exchange made a study of 4,000 customers. They found that the typical trader was male, about 45 years old (56% were between the ages of 35 and 55). Average earnings were in excess of $10,000 per year. 47% earned between $10,000 and $25,000. 39% earned in excess of $25,000. 54% of the 4,000 were professionals (doctors, lawyers, dentists, top management people or white collar workers). 68% had gone to college. 32% had not. 2,800 of the 4,000 also traded in stocks.

All speculators who are successful have capital available that is larger than the amount of margin required by the broker. I, personally, recommend you use only 75% of the total capital in your account and keep the other 25% in reserve.

Speculators buy (take long positions) or sell (take short positions) because they have formed an opinion that prices are about to move higher or decline. Those who are the most successful base their final decision on a close study of the fundamentals. They also use charts and certain trading techniques similar to those disclosed in this book.

YOU NEED NOT BE RIGHT ALL OF THE TIME

Most successful traders make mistakes. And some are wrong as many times as they are right. This is a very normal thing. When they are wrong, however, they take a small loss and get out. When they are right, they add to their positions and try to pyramid their profits.

This means you, too, will make mistakes. But, if you should be wrong as much as 50% of the time, you can still wind up each year with a good profit. Here is how.

Once you place an order to trade, you will either make a profit or you will lose. To be successful, you must make certain you take only small losses when you are wrong and take comparatively large profits when you are right. In this way, your total profits each year will always be larger than the total of your losses.

For an example, let us say you made 20 trades during the year. If you limit your losses on each trade to a maximum of 20% (including commissions) and aim for a minimum profit of 60% (after commissions), this is what you should have earned from 10 losses and 10 profits.

Assume an original investment of $2,000

		Loss	Profit
1st trade — loss 20%		$400	—
2nd trade — profit 60%		—	$1,200
3rd trade — loss 20%		$400	—
4th trade — profit 60%		—	$1,200
5th trade — loss 20%		$400	—
6th trade — profit 60%		—	$1,200
7th trade — loss 20%		$400	—
8th trade — profit 60%		—	$1,200
9th trade — loss 20%		$400	—
10th trade — profit 60%		—	$1,200
11th trade — loss 20%		$400	—
12th trade — profit 60%		—	$1,200
13th trade — loss 20%		$400	—
14th trade — profit 60%		—	$1,200
15th trade — loss 20%		$400	—
16th trade — profit 60%		—	$1,200
17th trade — loss 20%		$400	—
18th trade — profit 60%		—	$1,200
19th trade — loss 20%		$400	—
20th trade — profit 60%		—	$1,200
10 profits			$12,000
10 losses		$4,000	

Net profit for the year—$8,000—400% on $2,000

Occasionally, some of your losses will be more than 20%. But, to offset that, there will be times when some of the commodities you select will earn you a profit of 100% to 200% —sometimes more. When that happens, your net profits for the year could be larger than the 400% shown above. It all depends on your knowledge and timing. That is why it is so important to study and learn all you can from this book.

A 6¢ move in Pork Bellies, for example, will give you a profit of 211% on a single trade—instead of only 60%. A 5¢ move in Live Cattle will give you a profit of 196%. A 50¢ move in

Soybeans will give you a profit of 81%. An 8¢ move in Cocoa will give you 185%. A 5¢ move in Cotton will give you a profit of 123%. A 10¢ move in Copper will give you a profit of 163%. And a 30¢ move in Silver will give you a profit of 147%.

Such moves occur quite often every year. So you can see the potentials for profit in commodities are tremendous. All you need to do is—select the right commodity at the right time.

MOST TRADES ARE CARRIED
FOR ONLY A FEW WEEKS

Most professional traders in commodities hold a position for a few weeks—sometimes for only a few days. There are two reasons for this. One is — when a professional trader senses a "special situation," that commodity generally moves quite fast either up or down.

The second reason is—professional traders do not like to hold onto a position through a "trading market" where prices move up and down within a certain price level. They prefer to get out and wait for indications that prices will break out of such a trading range—either up or down. And, while some less active traders are waiting, they will look for another "special situation."

HOW COMMODITIES ARE TRADED

All commodities are traded on an open-auction type of market. This means that every order to buy or sell is clearly stated on the trading floor for all to hear. It is the fairest, most reliable and most efficient way to deal in commodity transactions.

This open-auction contrasts very strongly with the quiet and sometimes secret way that many stock market transactions are made. And, quite often, there will be "deals" made between certain specialists on the floor of the New York Stock Exchange.

With that in mind, you might find it interesting to read the comments made by a stock broker and investment advisor, Richard Ney. In his best-selling book, "The Wall St. Jungle," he points out some facts that few people know. He writes—

*Publisher—Grove Press, New York City, N.Y.

In this book, I will attempt to show that the state-ment, *"The stock market, by bringing together buy-ers and sellers from all over the world reflects their composite judgment of the present and future value of the stock"*—is false. I will try to show that a significant cause of the market's day-to-day fluc-tuating is, in fact, the manipulations of the special-ist. (from page 4)

Both the New York Stock Exchange and the SEC have failed to create the kind of approach that would contribute to the development of a sane and safe auction market. In the course of this book, we will acquire a new perspective on the meanings of such words as "stabilization" and "liquidity." And we will see that, far from stabilizing the market, the specialist system is so constructed that a specialist may exploit an emergency situation—or any an-nouncement, be it good or bad—to enrich his own account. (from page 7)

FACTORS THAT CAN CAUSE A CHANGE IN PRICE

The Commodity Exchanges do not set the price. They merely act as a meeting place for brokers. They record the price at which each trade is made each day. Those prices are then sent out all over the world through a special, elec-tronic wire service.

When more traders want to buy than want to sell, prices rise. When more traders want to sell than buy, prices decline.

There are two prices to consider when dealing in commod-ities. One is the cash price. The other is the futures price. The cash price is the result of present supply and demand for the actual commodity. A futures price, on the other hand, reflects what the cash price may be at some time — in the future.

If enough traders believe the information and statistics for a commodity will soon be fundamentally bullish, the prices on the futures market will be higher than the cash price.

If enough traders believe that fundamentals in a commod-ity indicate that prices in the future should be lower, the price of that commodity for future delivery may be less than the cash price.

The cash price and the price of the futures always approach one another as the month for delivery nears. The reason is —as the time required for storage, interest and insurance gets shorter, the cost of holding that commodity until delivery will decrease until, finally, there is little or no difference in price. In other words, if the "future" is to be delivered immediately, the commercial interests would rather have the cash commodity.

SEVERAL FACTORS AFFECT THE PRICE

Several factors affect the price of commodities. Some are long-range. Others are short-range. On a long-range basis, prices are influenced by—

1. The general level of all commodity prices.

2. The economy. Is it, generally speaking, inflationary or deflationary?

3. The value of money. As money declines in value (inflation), the price of commodities tend to rise. As money increases in value (deflation), prices tend to fall.

4. A change in the exchange rate between foreign countries may cause the exports or imports of a commodity to those countries to rise or fall.

5. New production techniques that increase the total supply and new methods of transportation can reduce the cost of production of a commodity. Prices, therefore, will tend to be lower. Or, during times of inflation, such improvements in production and transportation will keep prices at a reasonable level. Wheat, for example, sold at a lower price in 1972 than it did in 1950—in spite of a 55% rise in inflation. The same is true of bacon, eggs, sugar, cocoa, corn, coffee and many other commodities.

6. Competition. When prices of a commodity sell at very high levels, other commodities are sought as a substitute. If a certain grain, for example, is high-priced, a large amount of another grain may be used in the mixture of feed than would be used during times of normal prices. If Corn

gets too high in price, a larger proportion of Oats, Wheat or some other grain may be used. If the price of Pork Bellies gets too high, consumers look for other meats as a substitute and eat less bacon at that high price. If Cotton gets too high, cloth manufacturers look for synthetic yarns and materials to use as a substitute. If Soybean Meal gets too high, feed users look for cheaper protein substitutes.

7. Increase in production from under-developed countries. This is a long-range factor of growing importance. In the past, many under-developed countries were always short of certain commodities. Many of them could not support the needs of their people and had to import commodities. Now, with improved machines and production techniques, many of those under-developed countries may soon produce enough to create a larger world supply. When that occurs, it will tend to hold down the price of commodities produced in the countries that are better-developed.

SHORT RANGE FACTORS
THAT INFLUENCE PRICES

Some of the short-range factors that can cause a change in the supply and demand are—

1. Weather. This is one of the most important factors that can cause the price of perishable commodities to move up or down in price. Too much rain, too little rain, a prolonged drought, a tornado, hurricane and icy road conditions are some of the reasons why, over a few days or weeks, commodities like grains, livestock, cotton, orange juice, cocoa and sugar have wide and sometimes, sudden changes in price.

2. Planters and producers intentions. When prices of commodities are lower than normal, most producers will plan to reduce production. This helps to reduce the supply and prices will rise more easily. When prices are higher than normal, producers tend to produce more in hopes of

getting a high price for their products before prices decline.

3. Orders from foreign countries. When prices are low foreign buyers are inclined to buy more of that commodity. This extra amount of demand for a commodity can often help prices to move up faster than they normally would. And, of course, those same foreign countries may decide to buy less of a commodity when prices are high —or seek that commodity in some other country at a lower price. Substitutes may also be used on a temporary basis such as rice for corn, rape-seed for soybeans, rayon for cotton, beet sugar for cane sugar, sunflower seed oil for soybean oil, etc.

4. Strikes. A prolonged strike by any labor group concerned with transportation can slow down the distribution of commodities. Each strike must be appraised separately for its effect on the price of futures. If deliveries to a cash market are slowed down, this can cause the price of futures (especially in the nearby contacts) to rise because the demand for that commodity is greater than the actual supply at the point where it is marketed. If it concerns the export market and that commodity cannot be transported to another country, prices of futures can go lower because foreign buyers know the commodity cannot be delivered. Those foreign countries will, therefore, withhold their orders. They may look to other countries, or they will try to find substitutes for their supply. When that occurs, the country that hoped to sell for export will lose a certain amount of business. Prices will then tend to move lower and the supply may increase due to the loss of export business.

5. International developments. In all the commodities that move each year in international trade, it is wise to watch for unusual happenings in those foreign countries. Wars, for example, political upheavals, serious economic dis-

tress in one of those countries, unusual prosperity, or devaluation of the currency can cause a major change in the price.

6. Population increase. This seems to be a constant factor and helps to keep the demand for all commodities on the increase. Due to this population increase, all farmers and producers of commodities must continually search for and develop ways to increase their production to meet the needs of that increase in population. If, at any time, they are unable to do so, a shortage is created in that commodity and a steady increase in price can result until that shortage is overcome by an increase in production.

7. Crop disease and insect infestation. These factors occur in small amounts every year but, occasionally, they are severe. When they do occur, they can cause a decrease in production. An increase in the price of the commodity affected may then occur.

8. Estimates of supply and demand. As each month goes by, the estimates of supply and demand are revised. This helps to create prices in the market that reflect the true supply and demand situation. More supply means prices may go lower. And an increase in demand means prices may move higher.

That last fact caused the price of November soybeans to rise rapidly from around 3.40 per bushel in December, 1972 to more than $8.00 per bushel in July, 1973—a profit of $22,970 per contract.

A strong demand and a short supply also caused tremendous profits in such other commodities as Wheat, Corn, Live Cattle, Silver, Cocoa, Cotton, Copper, Eggs, Soybean Oil, Pork Bellies, Live Hogs and Iced Broilers.

A decrease in demand or an increase in supply will of course, cause a decline in prices. And large profits can be earned by those who learn how to sell "short" and buy back their short sale at a lower price. For example—November Plywood declined from a price of $154.00 in March, 1973 to less than $90.00 in July, 1973. For those who sold Plywood "short", that would mean a profit of $4,392 (439%) in only 5 months.

2

HOW TO BUILD THAT FORTUNE

One of the reasons why the rich get richer is—they like to make money. They find it fascinating. If you really like to make money, you will make it. If you don't enjoy making money—you will never make it. You will, instead, get tired easily, lose interest or find you don't care and that opportunity to get rich will never come.

There is no easy, sure way to build a fortune, but you can *build a fortune in commodities* if you learn to think like a professional and know what moves to make—at the right time. This means you must have the patience and the desire to study and learn to trade in a professional manner.

You don't need "luck" as you do in horse-racing, dice or roulette. You need—

Knowledge   —   Know-how   —   Courage

Knowledge is something you get from books and research reports. And you can gain that knowledge by reading, listening and learning. Know-how, like perfecting your swing in tennis or golf, comes from continuous practice and correcting your mistakes until you finally—*know how*. And your know-how will increase when you follow the principles and rules contained in this book.

Courage is something you either have or do not have. And a little courage is better than none. Every day a "special situation" is developing in some commodity that can help you *build a fortune.* When that opportunity comes, you must then have the courage to make a decision and act.

TRADING IN COMMODITIES IS A BUSINESS

Trading in commodities is a business. The study of the market, therefore, is important. But, if you like it, you will never consider it "work."

After you have carefully read and studied this book, you will find that trading in commodities is easier, more exciting and more practical than trading in stocks and bonds. In fact, the activity that goes on in the commodity markets make the stock market seem sluggish and dull by comparison.

If you like the action and the excitement of commodity trading, you will derive more fun and pleasure from trading in commodities than from any other business or hobby. But I suggest you start small. Trade lightly at first. Then trade more heavily after you have gained more knowledge and have the know-how necessary to be right more often than you are wrong.

The traders who are the most successful base their opinions on a close study of the fundamentals plus a knowledge of trading techniques.

There will be times when you will have to take a loss. At such times, you must have the courage and the intelligence to admit you are wrong—if you are. You must also have the humility and the willingness to be grateful for your good fortune when you are right. An arrogant, boastful attitude when you win will set you up for a loss. So you must have a continuous and able control over your emotions.

Sears-Roebuck, for example, may buy 10,000 suits and fail to sell them all at the price they would like to receive. But, generally, when they do not make a profit on each suit, they sell the reminder at 30% off, take the money that remains and try again.

Grocery stores buy meats, eggs, canned goods and other items at a certain price and hope to sell them at a profit. Sometimes, however, the price goes down. The result is— they have a loss on some of their purchases instead of a profit.

Such businesses do not quit. They continue to trade. They know there is always another day. And the best way to regain their loss is to stay in business. Commodity traders need to run their business in the same way.

The principle in the case of Sears-Roebuck and the grocery stores is to accept the losses whenever they occur and try to earn enough profits in the future to overcome those losses. By following this plan, they believe they can show a net gain at the end of each year.

Commodity traders, who understand the above point, realize that losses are, oftentimes, inevitable. But, if they are stubborn or allow their emotions, their pride or their ego to rule them, they will not be successful for long. And, of course, if they work for a store like Sears-Roebuck or a large super-market and display such emotions and ego, they will soon be out of a job. And that is the way it should be.

Learn or lose. Show courage or get out.

The trader who is wise will try to learn from others who have been successful in spite of many mistakes. And your money will grow if you learn a few sensible rules that professional traders have learned from long and hard experience. (Chapter 10 contains those rules and you should spend considerable time reading and memorizing those rules. Then follow them carefully until they become a part of your nature.)

Once you arrive at a decision on what to buy or sell—act. But, if you should find that your action did not pay off, reverse yourself—or—get out of the market.

The traders who are most likely to fail are those who enter the market unprepared—emotionally, psychologically and technically.

Doctors, lawyers, engineers, accountants and other professional men spend many years learning their profession. And their success is due to those years of study and intelligent preparation.

Those same men, however, will often enter a commodity market and neglect to use the good powers of judgement that are responsible for their success. Their analytical minds and their intelligence are left behind in their offices.

A successful business man will plan every detail, check on values and analyze all the ways he can earn a profit. At decision—making time, he may engage professional experts to help him. But, when it comes to trading in commodities —a business in which the profits per dollar invested are far greater than in his own business—he will, oftentimes, buy or sell merely because a broker may call and say, "The market is a good buy—or a sale." In other words, he will, too often, leave the possibility of a profit to luck or chance.

Most of the traders who lose money in commodities do so, primarily, for three reasons:

1. They don't know WHICH commodity to buy or

sell so they buy or sell the one they have heard a lot about — or one in which some friend or broker has an interest—and he joins them. He seldom checks, however, to make certain whether that friend or broker is right or wrong.

2. They don't know WHAT TIME to buy or sell. Here again they may be influenced by a friend or broker who may have bought or sold too soon. They find out, too late, that their friend or broker was right—at the wrong time.

3. They fail to control their emotions. They get hard—headed at times (even the best of professionals do this occasionally). Instead of being flexible, they may stay with a trade — even though they are wrong and try to fight it out. Their pride and their ego will not allow them to admit they are wrong.

LEARN TO CONTROL YOUR EMOTIONS

Besides knowledge of when to buy and when to sell, successful trading in commodities requires a continuous control over your emotions. In fact, the ability to control your emotions is the most important factor you must learn if you want to be a successful trader.

Unless you control your emotions, you will make many mistakes. Professionals know this. They also know the rules. And they try to follow those rules with prudence and care.

Many less experienced traders, however, take a position on impulse rather than reason. Then they wait to get "lucky". That is not speculating in the true sense of the word—that is gambling.

The truth is—you cannot become a "millionaire" trading in commodities. In fact, it is doubtful if you can become a successful "hundred-thousandaire"—year after year. The reason is—no human being can control his emotions well enough for that long a time.

Set your goal, therefore, at a realistic average earnings **of 30% per month—360% per year. If you can earn that** much from careful, conservative trading and repeat it for several years, you will be one of those successful traders who believe it is wiser to win and have something than "try for a million" and lose it all.

The commodity traders who succeed are those who know how to control their emotions. Like the professional football player, boxer or golfer, they are out to win. To do so, they will practice many days, if necessary, and analyze every situation to make certain they will be successful on that one big day when they decide to play.

If you understand your own strengths and weaknesses, you may find that the personality traits that help you to be successful in your present occupation may be a handicap when you trade in commodities.

Some people want the world to change for them. Others, who are wiser, realize that they are the ones who must change. This means you must be pliable. You must adjust your thoughts and actions to whatever happens in the market. As long as you do this, you can make progress. If you ignore it or try to prove how strong, smart and aggressive you are, you will surely lose.

To be one of those who win, you must know how to say, "It's my fault. I am to blame for my mistakes—not others."

If you are not willing to admit a mistake and you are reluctant to take a loss, you should not trade in commodities. You must always have the patience and the courage to accept your losses. Then look for a "special situation" to give you the profit you need to offset that loss. When you find one you like, take a position. If the market does move in your favor, you will quickly make up all of your losses and wind up each year with a net gain.

As you learned in Chapter 1, amateurs are those who do not want to take the time nor make the effort to become professionals. That is why amateurs in commodities so often lose money. They have heard that trading in commodities is a quick way to get rich. So they gamble. But gamblers are seldom winners for long.

To make money from the fast swings in commodities, you need to know how to win. From a practical standpoint, you should try to earn an average of approximately 30% per month—360% per year. If you think that a profit of $600 per month on an investment of $3,000 (or $1,500 on $5,000 —$3,000 on $10,000) per month is worth while having and you really want to have it — every month — then you must learn the rules and play the game like a professional. (The rules are given in Chapter 10. The techniques are given in Chapter 11, 12 and 13.)

Only winners are really congratulated. Professionals know this so they try to think, act and perform like a professional. And, most important, they know they must live by the rules in Chapter 10 that can help them become successful.

Only a foolish professional will ignore those rules. If he ignores the rules more than once, he may be out of the game.

Even if you are not a top flight professional, you will still earn more money than those who are amateurs because — amateurs are careless. They are lazy. They try to cut corners. They do not try to learn. And, worst of all, when they make a mistake, they blame someone else rather than themselves.

The first thing a professional does is—discipline himself. You, too, must do the same. And the stronger you are as an individual, the more you must discipline yourself. In commodity trading, the aggressive, human dynamo makes more **mistakes than the quiet, conservative and careful trader.**

When you trade conservatively, it is possible to start with very little money and build a small fortune. Once you become successful, however, new factors enter the picture. You tend to become egotistical. Then you may be inclined to believe you know more than you really do.

It happens to everyone. Especially to those who are inexperienced. But, when you become egotistical, the inevitable always happens. You get slapped down. You lose because you were so certain you would win.

You should neither be an aggressive powerhouse nor a coward. If you are the nervous type of individual who must continually call his broker for "advice" and moral support, you may lose more often than not, before you have a chance to really begin.

The characteristics that lead to success in commodity trading are:

Good judgment	Careful consideration
A flexible mind	Courage to act
Self-reliance	Perseverance
A humble attitude	Patience

Check each one of those eight carefully. If you already have all eight of those characteristics, you will soon be a professional. It will then be easier *to build a fortune in commodities*. If you are weak on any one or more of those characteristics, you should mark an X opposite them right now. Then make a steady and determined effort to develop those characteristics and use them in every part of your daily life.

A careful reading and study of the book, *"The Secret of Success"** will help you a great deal in this regard. I suggest you read this best-selling book. It will help you in many ways.

THE THREE WORST EMOTIONS

The three worst emotions are—*fear, hope and greed*. And they are most noticeable in amateur traders. As prices rise, they "hope" they will make money. When they see prices drop, they "fear" they will go lower. If they have a good profit, their "greed" says, "Hold on, you might get more."

FEAR

Fear will cause you to stay out of a commodity when, if you took a position (to buy or sell) the resulting move would make you rich. Fear will also cause you to act impulsively when reason and common sense would dictate otherwise.

You must learn to overcome the fear of loss. If you read the advertisements placed by such companies as Sears Roebuck, General Motors or the large supermarkets, you will find that many times during each year, they will sell merchandise at a lower price than they had hoped to get. But they never quit. They know that, in time, the present loss will be overcome by profits in the future.

They know it is a businesslike attitude to expect losses— not to fear them.

HOPE

There is no bigger fool than the one who "hopes" or "wishes" everything will turn out all right. So do not engage in "hope" or wishful thinking. The market is going to move in the direction it wants to—not the way you want it to. When you take a chance on something or trade on "hope" rather than on analysis and facts, you are certain to lose more.

*Best Books Inc., 3250 W. Irving Park, Chicago, Ill. 60618

If you follow all the rules in this book and your analysis says, "Yes, it is a time to buy or sell"—then you don't need **hope. You only need a stop loss in case your analysis was** not 100% correct.

Hope will never cause a market to move in your favor. So never rely on hope. Use careful analysis and judgment instead. And, especially, try to learn from the mistakes of others.

GREED

Greed can cause you to do things no intelligent, reasoning person would ever do. There are many stories that can be told about why greed is a foolish, emotional problem. The lessons they teach can all be summed up in these five points:

1. Don't try to get rich quick.
2. Don't be afraid to take small losses.
3. Let someone else have a profit.
4. Don't try to buy on the bottom—or sell on the top.
5. Take the largest profit you can—out of the middle—between the top and bottom.

BAD HABITS AND ATTITUDES
CAN CAUSE YOU TO LOSE

Bad habits and wrong attitudes can cause you to lose money. But losing money is a possibility that can happen in many activities—not only in commodities.

For example—a man can lose money in a business or even go bankrupt. Buying real estate at too high a price or in the wrong location is another. Gambling at Las Vegas or Monte Carlo. Betting on the horses. Buying General Motors stock at $105 per share in 1964 and watching it decline until, 10 years later, prices had declined to less than $35 per share.

All businesses can be learned. All problems can be overcome. You can learn *how to build a fortune in commodities* if you will observe certain common sense conservative rules that enable you to earn a profit while others, who are less careful, will lose.

Everyone cannot be a professional golfer, ball player, doctor or lawyer, but those who do study, practice and learn can certainly earn a larger income each year than those who are unwilling to take the time.

Fortunately, the large potential income is well worth the effort. No one guarantees a doctor or a lawyer $50,000 per year. He has to earn it. And no one will guarantee you will earn $50,000 per year trading in commodities. But it can be done. And this book should help you tremendously.

Doctors, lawyers, engineers and athletes say, "When you know what to do and what not to do, half the job is done."

If you have a large amount of money and become used to having it, your personality and your attitude tends to change —especially when you spend more time trading in commodities. The reason is—very few people can earn and possess a large amount of money. The majority tend to become greedy, arrogant or overly-aggressive. Those three attitudes, however, are contrary to the conservative methods that are so necessary for success in commodity trading.

In addition, when you become greedy, arrogant or overly-aggressive and try to double the large amount you have gained, the markets will, eventually, teach you an important lesson. You may lose at the very moment you were so certain you would win.

You will then learn why greed, arrogance and an overly-aggressive attitude are wrong. The market will act contrary to what you would like. It turns against you. You begin to act scared. Your losses increase. You may become stubborn and hold on because these three attitudes influence your decision. Prices may move further against you. The large amount of money you had will then grow smaller.

At that time, if greed and arrogance is still strong, you may buy more in a declining market (hoping to regain your loss) or you may sell in a rising market (hoping it will go lower). Now you are fully committed. Soon, you are short of money. You start to panic and lose your sense of balance. You find you have to "sell near the bottom of a move" or "buy near the top."

If you are wise, you soon realize why greed, arrogance and stubborness should never be brought into the market. Like a boxer who tries too hard for a knockout, you find you are knocked out yourself.

That is why you will find no "millionaires" in commodity

trading.

But this book is not designed to make you a millionaire. Instead it should help you learn how to be more successful so that, year after year, you can earn a larger amount of money.

Don't try to change the rules that have proved to be successful. Change yourself. The rules are basic and based on common-sense. They will remain long after you have gone. So, if you follow them, your fortune will increase. Disobey those rules and, eventually, you will become a loser.

Chapter 10 will give you those rules. Read them carefully.

ANALYZE YOUR MISTAKES

If you should lose money—and you will because everyone makes mistakes—analyze those mistakes and learn from them.

Very few traders do the right thing at the right time. Many of them trade in commodities, year after year, always hoping to make a lot of money. They fail to earn as much as they would like because they continue to make the same mistakes.

Mistakes in commodities are never fatal. They can, in time, be overcome. Fortunately, there is always another day. Another opportunity to make money will arise soon after your mistake was made. All you need is the capital and the courage to take advantage of a new "special situation" (See Chapter 9) when you see it developing on your charts.

If you learn from your mistakes, you will eventually become a success. That fact is as important in commodity trading as it is in the professions of medicine, chemistry, law, engineering or sports. After you understand why you lost, you can then begin trading again with the desire to do better the next time.

Loss of confidence is the greatest loss you can suffer. If you should lose some money, you must remember that, eventually, you can recover that loss and earn some more. But, once you lose your self-confidence, you are unable to reason clearly. You are afraid to buy or sell whenever you find a "special situation".

NEVER USE MORE THAN 75%
OF YOUR CAPITAL

If you are a beginner, never use more than 75% of the total amount you have deposited with your broker. The other 25% should be kept as a reserve. If you have $2,000 in your account, only use $1,500. If you have $5,000, only use $3,500. If you have $20,000, use only $15,000.

The reason is — you must always be conservative — not a plunger. And you may take some small losses from time to time. But, if you look for "special situations", the large profits you aim for will overcome those losses. And, eventually, you will have an increase in your capital.

TAKE SMALL LOSSES QUICKLY

You must be absolutely certain to keep your losses small. Only a masochist or a "born loser" likes to take large losses. So take small losses quickly. Don't wait for them to grow larger until all your capital is gone.

If you trade and the price near the close plus commission totals more than 20% close out your trade. Give your broker an order to "buy or sell at the close" (whichever it may be).

Take your small loss and get out. You will save a little on commission if it is a day trade. But, most important, you may find that the next day the market may go a little further in the same direction as the closing trend. That means, if you had stayed in the market, your loss that next day would be much larger. By getting out before the close—before prices move further against you—you actually save time as well as money.

The time is saved because, if you bought at a price of 2.56 in Wheat—or 44.50 in Pork Bellies—or 34.00 in Cotton and the price goes down to 2.50 or 42.50 or 31.00, you may have to wait a few days for the market to go back to where you bought it. And, of course, it may never go back to that level during the life of the contract.

The round trip down then back up is an unnecessary waste of time. That loss of time would be eliminated if you closed out your position the first day the market showed you had a loss of 20% or more.

There is another advantage of closing out a trade before it moves against you. You will have an opportunity to buy that same contract at a lower price. In a rising market, the extra advantage in price that you gain in this way helps you recover your small loss and, if you are right, it can add that much more profit to your next trade.

You could, for example, have 2 small losses that could total 60% per month, but, if you trade in "special situations" (see

Chapter 9) and have a net profit of 90% or more, your net gain for that month would be at least 30%.

STAY OUT OF BROKERS OFFICES

Stay out of broker's offices as much as possible. The traders who earn the largest amount of money are seldom seen in boardrooms. If they go into a broker's office, it is only for a few minutes.

Another point to remember is—don't tell anyone what you know or what you believe concerning a commodity or trade. Once you do, you upset your equilibrium. You tend to give importance to what you have said. If you repeat it often enough, you begin to believe it. Professional traders never do this. *They know that silence is golden.* They never tell anyone what they know or believe. They have learned it is always wise to keep flexible in their judgment so they can change their minds in as little as 10 minutes—if necessary—if the market should prove they are wrong. Their thoughts, therefore, are guided more by "Is it right?" rather than "This is right."

The most accurate judgments you will make are those made after you have spent much time alone—away from people and away from a broker's office. Market decisions are always better when they are made in a place where you can sit quietly and allow calm and considered judgment to help you.

TRADE IN ONLY ONE OR TWO COMMODITIES

Never trade in more than one or two commodities at a time. It is difficult to keep your mind calm and at ease when you try to sift through all the facts and information necessary to make a wise decision. While some commodities go up, others, at the same time, go down. And something always arises, at the wrong time, to cause confusion and upset your judgment.

DON'T RELY ON TIPS OR ADVICE FROM OTHERS

Don't rely upon tips or advice from others. Use some judgment of your own. Other people and advisory services can only point out *a possibility for profit.* In the final analysis, you must solve your own problems.

You don't know it all. I don't know it all. And especially beware of the man who thinks he knows it all. Too often, you will find — *he knows not that he knows not.*

The greatest satisfaction in life comes from things you personally do on your own initiative and judgment. If you listen to rumor and opinions or "wait for news" before you decide to trade, you may miss many good opportunities.

Speculation in commodities requires the same kind of study and care that is required for successful speculation in real estate, antiques, used cars or building a new business.

Be a "lone wolf." Keep you trading plans a secret. And, above all, ignore the "advice" and opinions expressed by customers who sit in boardrooms. Most of them will confuse you. They usually trade on "hope" and "wishes"—and very few of them make money.

Of the estimated, 1,500,000 traders (in 1972) in the commodity markets, less than 30% have made a careful and prolonged study of those markets. The other 70% enter the market from time to time because they have received "a tip" or heard some news that caused them to believe a certain commodity is a good buy or a good sale.

Based on that tip, they "take a chance". They "hope" that commodity will move—up or down in their favor. But their lack of knowledge can prove costly—especially when they accept that tip and buy in spite of the fact that commodity may be at a price near the top of an up-move or sell near the bottom of a long decline.

WHAT ABOUT BULLISH OR BEARISH NEWS?

If you feel a news report is going to be bullish and it does come out bullish, that is no guarantee the market will move up. Many times, if a bullish report is expected, the market will open a little higher or almost unchanged. It may even open lower if the news has already been discounted.

And, of course, if you feel a report is going to be bearish and it actually comes out bearish, that is no guarantee the market will continue to sell off. The market may actually open steady, hold firm or move up—depending on where the market might be in relation to the long-range fundamentals.

OVERTRADING WILL COST YOU MONEY

Overtrading will cost you money — every time. Many traders feel that, after they have made a few successful trades, they can then be less conservative, trade more heavily and commit all of the money in their margin account.

A truly prudent investor, however, never puts his last dollar

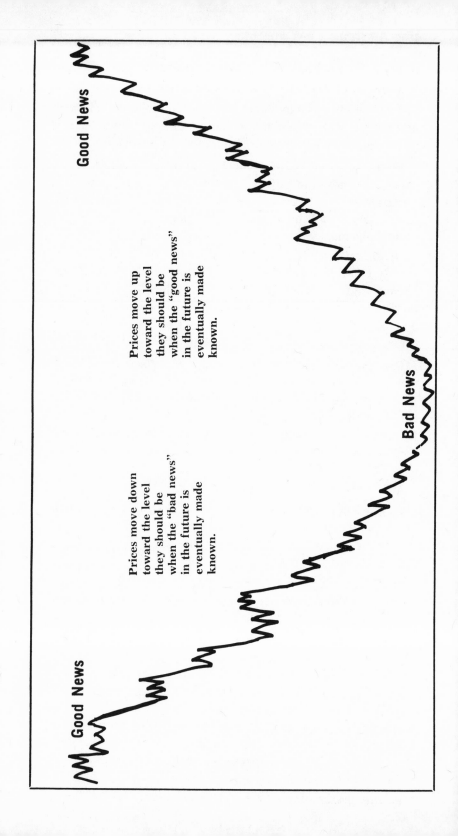

to work. He knows there is always a risk involved.

Commodity markets, like everything else that goes on in life, is not certain. Weather conditions, wars, strikes, large and sudden purchases from foreign countries, dumping of a commodity for one reason or another by some large commercial interest and so on, often occur overnight. That is why you need to protect yourself at all times.

When you believe you know it all—then is the time when you stand to lose it all.

A good business man, in commodities or any other business is basically humble, always flexible, open-minded, able to change his viewpoint, looks for opportunities and is always aware that whatever he owns may not be sold at a profit.

If you like to bet on the horses or roll the dice at Las Vegas, you may feel you need to keep active when trading in commodities. If you do, your broker may be the only one to profit.

You cannot win if you feel you must trade in the market every day. There will be many times when you will need a rest. And this inactivity, on the sidelines, will help you gain a new perspective.

If you are out of the market, you will find it easier to see one or more "special situations" that can offer you a large potential for profit.

PRICES MOVE UP OR DOWN TO JUSTIFY THE NEWS

Prices of all commodities move up or down to justify the news at some time—in the future. If the news concerning a commodity has been bad for several weeks, the market will tend to make a bottom for a move towards higher prices. Why? Because in a few more weeks or months, the news will be better and prices will rise to justify that news.

If the news for several weeks or months has been good, prices will make a top then move down. Conditions will change because producers, processors and suppliers, will find ways to increase the supply, or they will decide to buy less of that commodity at such a high price. They may also try to let the supply increase so they can buy whatever they need at lower prices.

As prices move down, the news becomes less bullish and traders find it easier to believe a bear trend is underway. (See the Chart on the opposite page.)

The principle to remember is this. The market price of all commodities will move up or down toward a level that makes "the news" come true so that when the good or bad news eventually comes, the price will justify that news.

As a market dealing in "futures," that is the way it should be. If the news you read has been discounted by the market a few days or even a few weeks in advance of the day the news is released, prices may turn around and move in the opposite direction.

WHEN REPORTS ARE KNOWN THEY ARE USUALLY DISCOUNTED

Commodity markets tend to discount known factors and adjust to conditions that might be anticipated in the future. Government reports, for example, are released during the growing season. Yet, many times, a market will go up in spite of a bearish report or go down in spite of a bullish report. The reason is — professional traders and the large commercial interests have already analyzed the fundamentals. They have expected such a report and they have "discounted it in the market."

Normally, when big deliveries are made on the nearby futures contracts, it is considered bearish. But the market may not go down. It has already accepted that situation and discounted its importance.

To understand futures prices in relation to supply and demand, statisticians use a balance sheet. They add the carryover of a particular commodity from the previous year to the new production. This gives the supply available at the beginning of the season. From this total, exports and domestic use are deducted. Every month, inventory checks are taken. These figures give all those interested in that commodity an estimate of the actual supply on hand at that time. They also help to gauge the rate of disappearance. If the rate of disappearance is slow, prices will move very little. If the rate is fast or picking up, then prices may move higher much faster than they normally would.

Generally, if a shortage is anticipated, the rise in price may be somewhat larger than the percentage of deficit. For example, if the shortage is expected to be around 10%, prices could rise as much as 30% higher than they normally would rise. A 20% deficit could cause prices to rise as much as 60% higher than normal. A 10% increase in supply could cause prices to decline as much as 30% below the normal amount of decline. **A 20% increase in supply could cause prices to decline** as much as 60% below normal.

That point should be remembered because it helps to explain why commodity prices always move farther—up or down —than they should. In an up-trend, the "shorts" buy frantically in an effort to get out. This causes the market to move to a point where it is "overbought." And, in a down-trend, the longs try to get out before prices go lower. This causes prices to decline to a point where the market is "oversold."

Prices generally move sharply higher during a shortage of supply. Eventually, after such a rapid advance, prices will drop very fast because the higher prices cause the demand to fall off. Or, after the sharp decline, prices will rally and move higher because commercial interests who look for reasonable prices will cause an increase in demand for that commodity.

If you are alert to those potential price changes, you can often take a position (long or short) which can prove to be very profitable when the change in fundamentals ultimately becomes known by other traders.

BASE YOUR DECISIONS ON FACTORS THAT ARE 60% FUNDAMENTAL AND 40% TECHNICAL

When you decide to trade, your decisions should be based on factors that are 60% fundamental and 40% technical. This means, you must remember that commodity markets will tend to move in the direction—up or down—to justify the long-term factors of supply and demand, potential production, inventories at terminal markets, potential use of that commodity, exports and what may happen to the price of competing commodities. (See page 38.)

If the long-term fundamentals indicate that prices — in the future — will be bullish, prices may decline, temporarily, due to technical considerations. That is why "charts" are so important. They indicate why, sometimes, you should ignore the fundamentals and buy or sell for a short-term move in the opposite direction.

Or, if you do not want to sell, charts can help you be patient and wait for lower prices. In other words, you can be bullish, based on the long-term fundamentals, but "short" on a temporary basis due to the technical considerations based on your reading of the charts.

If you should ever feel confused due to the above bullish fundamentals and short-term weakness shown in the charts, then it is wise to "stay out of the market." Leave that commodity alone until a clearer picture develops or the charts indicate that a purchase is indicated. The short-term activity of the charts should show support on the decline and indicate the possibility of a move toward higher prices to fulfill the **higher price—in the future—the bullish fundamentals have** given.

The reverse, of course, is true when you want to sell in a declining market. If you believe the market should be selling at a lower price in a few months, but the charts show that a technical rally is due, you must make one of two decisions: (1) whether you want to hold your short position even though prices move up, temporarily, against you or (2) whether you should take a profit on your short sale in an effort to sell at a little higher price after the rally has taken place.

You will learn in Chapter 11 how to profit from the changes in trend that occur in every commodity .

LEARN HOW TO SELL SHORT

To be successful in commodity trading, you must **learn how** to "sell short"'. If you trade only for an up-move, you may be out of the market as much as one-half the year because prices of commodities (like stocks) go down as well as up.

You sell a commodity "short" when you feel that prices may go down and you believe you can buy that commodity at a lower price. If you sell short at the beginning of a bear market, your profits can increase at a rapid rate. Why? Because prices always go down faster than they go up.

The reason is—prices have to be pushed up. There has to be many more buyers than sellers and those buyers must be willing to pay the higher prices. In a declining market, however, prices drop easily and fast. As an increasing number of sell orders come into the trading pits, buyers stand aside. They wait or refuse to buy—except at lower prices. (See the long-range charts on each major commodity in Chapters 4, 5 and 6. You will see these sharp and comparatively fast declines after a long rise.)

The one rule to remember is—when selling "short"—never try to sell "short" if prices remain in an uptrend. You have no way of knowing how much higher the market may move.

The "moving averages" explained on page 145 will help you "time" your sale so that you can sell much closer to the top of a bull move.

After a long up-trend, prices may churn about without making much headway. Take a good look at the fundamentals. They may indicate that prices should soon be lower in order to justify what those fundamentals may be—in the future.

If bearish fundamentals are due in a few more weeks or months, sell the market "short"—especially if the "moving averages" that appear on your charts indicate the possibility of a decline. Then follow through—all the way down.

When you examine your charts, you will see "resistance levels" at lower prices. As those resistance levels are broken, sell some more "short". Or, after a decline, sell some more short the third day after the market has had a rally.

Buy back your "shorts" only when the market reaches a point where enough buying power comes in to stop the market from going lower. The 4-day, 9-day and 18-day "moving averages", explained on page 145, will help you make this decision more easily.

And, especially, study the fundamentals. If the fundamentals indicate that, in a few weeks the news will be more bullish than it has been during the past few weeks and the demand for that commodity may soon increase, a bottom may be made —at least temporarily—and a rise in prices should begin.

If you should buy and go long, however, after a bear market ends, your profits will not be as large nor will they come fast. It takes several weeks to build a base for a good bull move to get underway.

While that base for a bull move is building, you will, generally, earn much larger profits by trading in one or more "special situations". (See Chapter 9 for more information on "special situations".)

3

THE IMPORTANCE OF HEDGING

Futures markets were set up in all of the major commodities to create a means whereby farmers, producers, feedlot operators, shippers, manufacturers of finished products such as cotton mills, chocolate manufacturers, candy producers, silver and copper manufacturers, cereal companies, meat packers, exporters and other commercial interests can protect themselves against a 'sudden and drastic rise or decline in price before they can complete a sale for their products.

The way they protect themselves is called—*hedging*.

Hedging is—taking a position in the futures market equal to but opposite the amount of commodities a hedger plans to buy or sell on the cash market.

Hedgers are people or companies engaged in any phase of the commodity business. They all have a large investment in plant and equipment. They do not speculate. Their main interest is to earn a reasonable profit on the amount of money they have invested in their business.

They know that each day the price of commodities will move up or down to reflect the influence of orders coming into the Exchange from all over the world. And those prices will vary according to the supply and the demand.

Commercial interests, therefore, find it necessary to place hedges (sell short) and buy back those hedges (liquidate their position) when they want to protect their profits in the commodities they produce or market. This eliminates the major portion of the speculative risk and helps the hedgers feel more comfortable.

'The market orders of those commercial interests have a great influence on the market. In fact, the cumulative amounts they buy or sell are much larger than the cumulative amounts that are bought or sold by thousands of small speculative traders.

As a management tool, the futures market helps to lower the cost of doing business, improves the financial and competitive position of a company and benefits the ultimate consumer through, generally, more stable prices.

TWO KINDS OF HEDGES

Hedging is taking a position in the futures market opposite to the position taken in the cash market. There are, therefore, two kinds of hedges. The "selling hedge" and the "buying hedge".

When a commercial interest owns a quantity of the cash commodity or buys a quantity of a commodity on the cash market, his main interest is to earn a profit from what he owns. But he has a problem. The price may change. It may go up or down—in a few days or even overnight. Obviously, if the price goes down before he can sell his inventory at a profit, he will lose money rather than gain. To protect himself against that possible decline in price, he will immediately sell an equal amount of that commodity "short" on the futures market.

That is called a "selling hedge". He is then long the cash commodity and hopes to make a profit from its sale. While he holds his cash commodity, the "short hedge" protects the value of his inventory against a possible decline in the cash price.

If the price of the cash commodity should decline, he would lose a substantial amount of money on his inventory. But the decline in the price of his "short hedge" in the futures market would protect him against that decline in the cash market because the decline in the price of the futures market would be approximately the same as the amount of decline in his cash—one decline would help to offset the other. His actual loss, if any, would then be small.

If, however, the futures rose to a higher price, he would have a loss in his "short hedge." But the value of his cash inventory would also rise. The profit gained on his cash inventory would help to offset the loss in the futures market.

When the "selling hedge" is placed on a distant delivery and the price of that distant month is higher than the nearby month, the higher price of the futures market helps to pay most of the storage costs, interest and other costs of the hedger.

A "selling hedge" is placed when a commercial interest has

something to sell and feels a commodity may soon drop in price. If the cash price is lower than he hoped it would be at the time he markets his commodity, he can regain that loss (or most of it) by buying back his "short hedge".

The "buying hedge" is the opposite of the short hedge. It is used to protect a commercial interest against a possible increase in the price on the cash market.

For example—an exporter may receive a request to deliver a certain commodity at a fixed price several months later. He writes an order and agrees to deliver that commodity at that price.

When he writes this order, he has two problems. First, he does not own that commodity. He is, therefore, "short" because he has not acquired enough of the cash commodity to fill his order. Second, he is not certain whether the price of that commodity will be higher or lower at the time of delivery.

Since he has promised to deliver that commodity at a fixed price, he may find he has to pay more for the cash commodity than the price at which he promised to deliver it. In that case, he would lose money.

But commercial interests cannot afford to gamble. A few large losses and they would be out of business. To protect themselves against that possibility, a farmer or commercial interest will contract, in the futures market, for a "buying hedge". He will then be long the same amount of that commodity as the amount he has promised to deliver.

If the cash market should rise before he has a chance to acquire the amount of the commodity he needs, he will then have a profit on his "buying hedge". This profit will then help to offset the loss he will have to take when he finds he must pay a higher price for the cash commodity than the price he wanted to pay when he promised to deliver it.

Sometimes the profit from a hedge is larger than expected. At other times, the profit may be less than the amount that could have been received if those farmers, processors and exporters had stayed only with the cash market. But those who use the futures markets to hedge—either long or short—find it is wise to do so because the hedge will help to protect them against any major change in price.

In brief, whenever the futures market is used as a hedge, the loss on one side of the market (futures against cash) is usually offset by a profit on the other side. In effect, the hedge (whether it is a long or a short position) gives the commercial interest the protection he needs against any drastic or sudden change in price before he has had a chance to complete his sale in the cash market.

The "buying hedge" eliminates the need for commercial interests to build or rent additional storage facilities. This reduces the need to tie up working capital over long periods of time. The funds of those commercial interests are, therefore, used only for productive purposes.

THERE IS NO PERFECT HEDGE

Hedging is not an automatic way to make money. And there is no perfect hedge. For a hedge to be perfect, the cash price and the futures price should move up and down together at the same time. That seldom happens.

The hedge, however, is not designed to give 100% protection. Instead, it protects against a sudden and drastic change in price—and they often occur. A hedge, therefore, is like car insurance. You never need it except in an emergency. Even after the accident, the car owner does not receive all of the money he needs. Most insurance policies have a $50 or $100 deductible clause and that amount is never returned to the owner of the policy.

HEDGING HELPS TO CREATE ORDERLY MARKETS

Hedging on a futures contract gives commercial interests a more certain way to assure themselves of a potential profit in advance. It also helps all those individuals and businesses interested in commodities to earn more profit while operating on a small mark-up.

In fact, hedging can be an important help in these days of strong competition. But, to be successful in hedging, it takes an intensive study of the market, knowledge of a commodity, transportation costs and general economic conditions.

Without the orderly marketing process made possible by the futures market and the speculators, prices of commodities would be too high when supplies are short. And they would sink too low when supplies are more abundant.

The price the consumer would pay for such commodities would, therefore, be much greater than under present methods that use the futures markets to create a hedge to eliminate that price uncertainty and make it easier for a company doing business in commodities to earn a profit.

Producers want to be assured of a profitable selling price and purchasers want to protect themselves against unforeseen rises in cost. A futures contract, therefore, benefits them both.

When a processor or a distributor buys a futures contract, it makes it easier for them to estimate finished costs, set more competitive selling prices and anticipate profits. Trading in futures gives such business men more peace of mind than they could have without it.

A large grain elevator, for example, may store as much as 5,000,000 bushels of grain in their elevators. During the harvest season, most of their elevator space is filled. If the grain they hold in storage should go up or down only 5¢ per bushel, that change in price would result in a gain or a loss of $250,000. A 10¢ change in price would be $500,000. And a 20¢ change would be $1,000,000.

By hedging the value of their inventory in the futures market, such a company can maintain a larger inventory. Then they can borrow against that inventory. This allows them to operate on a smaller amount of actual capital. But, with such a large amount of grain in their possession, they can earn a large amount of money with only a small mark-up.

As an example, let us assume that a grain elevator owner buys 5,000 bushels of grain on September 1st at $1.50 per bushel. To protect against a decline in price, he will then sell 5,000 bushels of that grain "short" on the futures market.

His order will, generally, read, "Sell 5,000 May short—at the market" This will do two things: (1) It will protect him against a loss on the cash grain he holds if the cash price should go down and (2) It will enable him to earn money from the primary source of his income—the storage charges he must ask for storing the grain.

At a later date, (usually before the May delivery date), he will sell the grain to a processing firm. This will liquidate his cash position. At the same time, he must get out of his "short hedge" so he buys back the 5,000 bushels of May he sold short as a hedge. His profit or loss is determined by the difference in the sale and the purchase price.

The above explanation applies to all commodities. Simply substitute the word—Cotton, Cocoa, Silver, Eggs, Live Cattle,

Hogs, Plywood, etc. for the word grain.

BANKERS LIKE HEDGES

Bankers like hedges because they know it takes a lot of money to finance a large inventory of any commodity. And they like to do business with farmers, processors, warehouses and exporters of commodities who have a knowledge of the futures markets.

As a general rule, bankers will loan up to 90% of the value of a commodity that is hedged, but only 50% to 75% when it is not hedged.

They know that when a commodity is "hedged", it is safer to loan money on that commodity because it can provide the borrower with price security for a loan that might, otherwise, be risky without it.

When a commercial interest uses a hedge as price protection, he can triple or quadruple his profits. Here is how.

Commercial banks will loan up to 90% of the total value of the cash inventory that is held by an elevator, processor, exporter or manufacturer. This means that, with $20,000 of his own capital, he can handle up to $200,000 of a commodity. With $50,000 of his own capital, he can handle up to $500,000, and so on.

If he were to handle $200,000 of inventory, his profits would be figured on that $200,000 when it is sold—less the interest paid to the bank for the loan and, of course, the extra cost of handling $200,000 of the commodity instead of only $20,000. The result, after deducting those costs, would give that commercial interest a profit three to four times larger than the profit he would have on the smaller amount of only $20,000.

The bank, therefore, is an important aid towards helping all dealers in comodities secure extra profits. But the bank wants protection for the large amount of money it loans against that inventory. To gain that protection, the bank will insist on a "hedge" in the futures market.

As more farmers and other commercial interests understand the futures markets, there will be a greater interest in hedging and the open-interest in commodities will increase tremendously. It is hoped, therefore, that this book will help all those interested in commodities to understand more about the importance of the futures markets and give them the confidence they need to trade more profitably.

There are trained specialists in more than 3,000 commercial banks thoughout the United States who loan money on commodities.

If you are a farmer, processor or any other type of commercial interest who needs to know more about hedging for either price protection or for securing a loan you can write to the Commodity Hedging Department of any large bank in any major city. They will either help you find the best way to hedge whatever you have to market or they will give you the names of banks that can work with you in your area.

4

BASIC FACTS ABOUT THE GRAINS

This chapter will help you understand the basic facts about the grains. If you need more information, you can get it from any commodity broker. Or you can write to the sources that prepare specific reports or subscribe to magazines that devote their time to a specific commodity. (See Chapter 15 for sources of information.)

WHEAT

Wheat is grown in almost every country around the world. The total supply of wheat—world-wide—was 12 billion 500 million bushels in 1973 with a total value of over $30 billion. In the United States, 1,640 billion bushels were harvested. The total market value was over $5 billion.

There are two planting times for wheat. The first is Winter Wheat. This crop is planted in the United States between September 1st and October 20th. After lying dormant during the winter, it is harvested late in May through the months of June and July. The other is Spring Wheat. This is sown as early as the ground can be worked in the spring. Harvest of Spring Wheat begins in July and continues through August and September.

Hard Red Winter Wheat and Hard Red Spring Wheat contain large quantities of gluten and is used, primarily, to make flour for bread. Most of the Hard Red Wheat is grown in the States of Kansas, Oklahoma, Texas, Nebraska, Montana, North Dakota and South Dakota. Soft Red Winter Wheat has less protein content and is used, primarily, to make pastry, crackers, biscuits, cakes and similar products. This wheat is grown in the states that lie East of the Mississippi River.

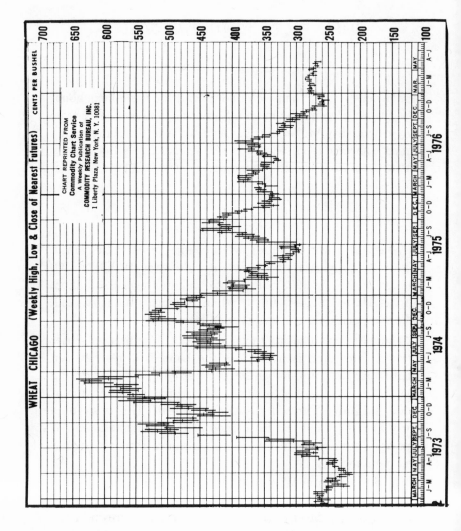

WHEAT CHICAGO (Weekly High, Low & Close of Nearest Futures) CENTS PER BUSHEL

CHART REPRINTED FROM
Commodity Chart Service
A Weekly Publication of
COMMODITY RESEARCH BUREAU, INC.
1 Liberty Plaza, New York, N.Y. 10081

Durum wheat is used to make macaroni, spaghetti and similar products. It is grown mostly in the state of North Dakota and southern Manitoba, Canada.

The supply of wheat each year consists of the wheat that remains from the previous season (the carryover), plus the production from the harvest and the imports. Imports of wheat into the United States, however, are very small and consist mainly of seed.

The deliverable contract in Chicago is the Soft Red winter wheat. Hard Red winter wheat is deliverable on Kansas City contracts. Hard Red spring wheat is deliverable in Minneapolis. When prices in Chicago are high and transportation costs plus an extra profit can be secured, the Hard Red winter wheat and the Hard Red spring wheat can both be delivered in Chicago to take advantage of those higher prices.

If the price of wheat is cheap compared to the price of feed grains, farmers may feed wheat to livestock. This can cause a faster disappearance than normal and, thereby, help to reduce the supply.

Farmers often expect prices to remain high in the year that follows a bull market. They are then inclined to hold onto their wheat and hope for better prices. If those better prices do not come, this holding action can cause prices to decline faster than normal when those farmers sell their wheat at prices less than they had expected to receive.

Government actions will, oftentimes, affect the price of wheat. The most important government influences are the price support program, government loans, diversion payments and attempts to cut back or increase the amount of acreage planted in wheat.

The availability of storage space and the facilities available to move the wheat to market by freight cars or trucks can also affect the price of wheat temporarily. If wheat moves to market too slowly due to transportation difficulties, prices will remain high for a longer period than normal. If wheat can be moved faster to market, it can cause prices to decline due to the increased number of hedges coming into the market.

CORN

The production of corn is a big and important business. World-wide production is over 15 billion bushels. Approximately 50% or an average of 8 billion bushels (valued at $18

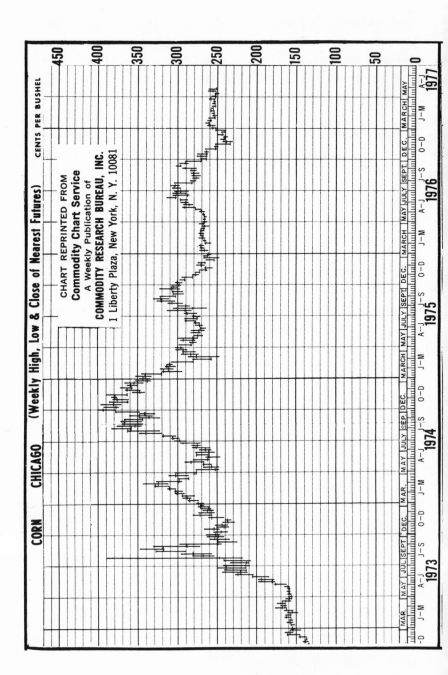

CORN CHICAGO (Weekly High, Low & Close of Nearest Futures)

CENTS PER BUSHEL

CHART REPRINTED FROM
Commodity Chart Service
A Weekly Publication of
COMMODITY RESEARCH BUREAU, INC.
1 Liberty Plaza, New York, N. Y. 10081

billion) is produced in the United States.

85% to 90% of the corn production is used for feed for hogs, poultry, beef and dairy cattle, turkeys and sheep. The remaining 10% to 15% (about 500 million to 750 million bushels) goes to the corn-processing industry or is exported.

In its final form, corn becomes beef, bacon, ham, turkey and chicken. Other products that result from the feeding of corn are milk, eggs and butter.

Corn is also used for industry. One is for starch. This is used in the paper, textile, laundry and food industries. Corn oil, another by-product of corn is used as an oil for cooking and a base for mayonnaise, margarine and salad dressing. Corn is also used to make alcohol and bourbon whiskey.

Corn is grown in almost every state, but more than 75% of the total production comes from the "corn belt" states of Iowa, Illinois, Minnesota, Indiana, Nebraska, Ohio, Missouri, Wisconsin and South Dakota. It is generally planted from April 20th to June 1st. And early planting helps to increase the yield. Harvest begins around July 20th and usually ends near the end of October.

Weather can have a good or bad affect on the yields of corn. Hot and dry weather during July and August can damage corn and cause a smaller yield. If the rainfall during July and August is higher than normal (but not too wet), it will increase the yield of corn. If the rainfall is below normal, especially during July, the yield may be less. If the weather during August is unusually hot for several days, it will tend to reduce the yield. Corn may also be hurt by an early frost in September.

It is wise, therefore, to watch the weather. If the yield may be less than the forecast made in April, prices may rise during July and part of August. If the yield may be larger than forecast, then corn prices may decline more than usual during August.

Most corn is generally kept on the farms after harvest to dry. Then it is put into storage. Corn moves to market slowly. It generally reaches a peak during November through January. Feed demands are heavy during the winter months, especially from February through April. Pressure on prices is generally light during that time and prices tend to rise from February until late May or June. Then hedging comes in as harvest time approaches and prices tend to move down.

During most years, corn will experience an average rate of production and an average rate of demand. Prices, therefore, will tend to move up and down during those years in a logical, somewhat easy to forecast fashion. Occasionally, there will be years when production will be too high or too low. If the production and the carryover during any year are going to be high, commercial interests and speculators are less likely to buy. Prices will then tend to be lower than usual and stay low longer. And, when prices start to move up, they will not move up as fast nor as far as in years when production is not as great.

If the production and carryover is going to be smaller than usual, the commercial interests and speculators buy as soon and as heavily as they can. Prices then move up quite rapidly. They reach their high and stay at that high level longer than usual during normal years. But this high level of prices creates a good opportunity for short sales because, as soon as news comes out that production will be back to normal once again, prices will drop and continue to drop as long as production does increase the supply to create a more normal market.

As a major part of the food-grain supply, corn makes up about one-fourth of the total amount of feed concentrates. An estimate of the total number of hogs, cattle, poultry and sheep can help you know how much demand there might be for the corn that is produced.

High livestock prices when corn is cheap will encourage farmers to feed more corn to their livestock. It will also encourage them to increase the numbers of hogs, cattle and poultry.

The amount of corn each animal will consume is approximately in this relationship. 8 cattle will consume as much as 11 hogs and 1,200 chickens. From those figures, you can estimate the demand for corn once you know the total numbers of cattle, hogs and poultry on farms.

If the total number of livestock and poultry is large, they will consume larger quantities of corn, but if the total number should be smaller than usual during one or two years, there may be a larger surplus of corn (unless exports should increase at that time). Prices then will be lower than normal until larger numbers of livestock and poultry are raised.

Each month, the USDA publishes feed price ratios for

live cattle and live hogs. The hog-corn ratio for example, can be estimated by dividing the market price of live hogs by the price of corn. In July 1974 the average price of live hogs was 41.00. July corn averaged $3.20 per bushel. This created an unfavorable hog-corn ratio of 12.8. This ratio means that for every $1.00 amount of corn fed to hogs, the farmer would net $1.28 from the sale of his hogs. Not enough profit.

To break even, a farmer needs a hog-corn ratio of at least 14.5. If the hog-corn ratio is below 14.5, the farmer would earn more income from the sale of his corn than from feeding it to his hogs. This would tend to decrease the number of hogs.

Feed-livestock ratios, therefore, are a good indication of the potential demand for corn. But, if there is a possibility that hogs may be selling at higher prices in six months, this can create a situation where farmers would feed more corn to hogs to increase their weight. The demand for corn would then be greater and the price of corn could rise more than usual.

The United States is a large exporter of feed grains so it is necessary to watch the production of feed grains in other countries, especially Argentina, Australia, Canada, France, South Africa and Russia. If production in those countries should increase, it will decrease the need for exports from the United States.

Demand for corn from foreign countries depends a great deal on the price. When the supply of corn in the United States is short and prices are high compared to the price offered by other exporting countries, exports from the United States will decline. And, when production and supply are larger than normal, prices are generally lower and other countries will then be more inclined to buy United States corn.

Each year, the government sets a farm-loan price. It also states a price at which it will sell the supplies it holds on the open market. These two government influences may cause prices to move up or down at three important price levels:

1. At harvest time, the government sets a farm loan price so that corn producers may be willing to place their crop under that loan. This price level forms a sort of "floor" under which prices are not likely to go. The movement of corn into government loan tends to decrease the free market supply. If

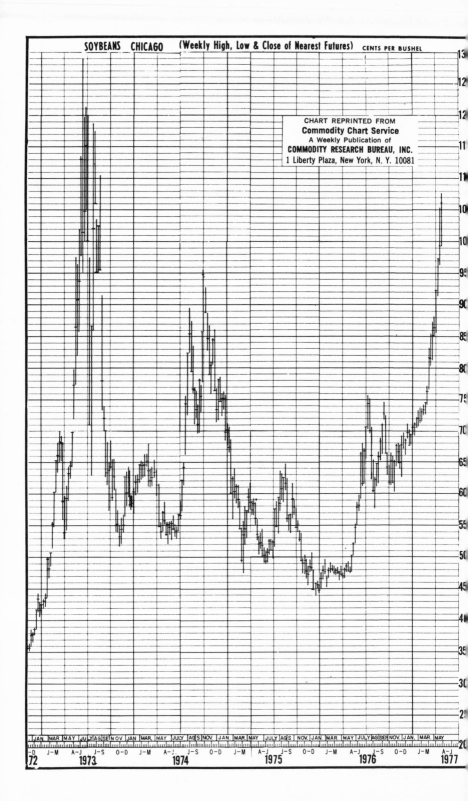

SOYBEANS CHICAGO (Weekly High, Low & Close of Nearest Futures) CENTS PER BUSHEL

CHART REPRINTED FROM
Commodity Chart Service
A Weekly Publication of
COMMODITY RESEARCH BUREAU, INC.
1 Liberty Plaza, New York, N. Y. 10081

the supply of corn is large, that can cause the price to rise to the loan level.

2. The government may set a market price high enough over the loan to cover the cost of redemption, including the interest on the loan.

3. When the government sells its stocks of grain on the open market, that price becomes a temporary "ceiling". It is effective in years when there is a short supply.

SOYBEANS

Soybeans are one of the most popular commodities for traders. During 1971, an estimated $48.2 billion of soybeans were bought and sold on the Chicago Board of Trade—and that figure is likely to grow larger for many years as the production of soybeans continues to increase in an effort to satisfy the great demand for this versatile and valuable commodity.

Soybeans are grown in more than 20 states, but production is, primarily, in the corn belt states plus Arkansas and Mississippi. Harvest begins in September and ends in early November.

Soybeans and soybean products are one of the United States leading exports because the demand for soybeans, soybean meal and soybean oil keeps increasing as more people and more countries around the world realize the great value of soybeans as a food for both humans and animals. Approximately 45% of the crop each year is exported. Western Europe buys approximately one-half of the export. Japan buys about one-fourth and Canada buys about one-sixth.

A bushel of soybeans weighs about 60 pounds. When the beans are crushed, the process gives approximately 47 pounds of meal, 11 pounds of oil and about two pounds is lost as waste.

The difference between the value of soybeans and the combined value of the soybean oil and meal is called the gross processing margin. Approximately 25c per bushel is needed for soybean processors to earn a good profit.

If the price of soybeans move higher but the oil and meal prices do not, soybean processors may then cut back on their crushings until the gross processing margin is more favorable

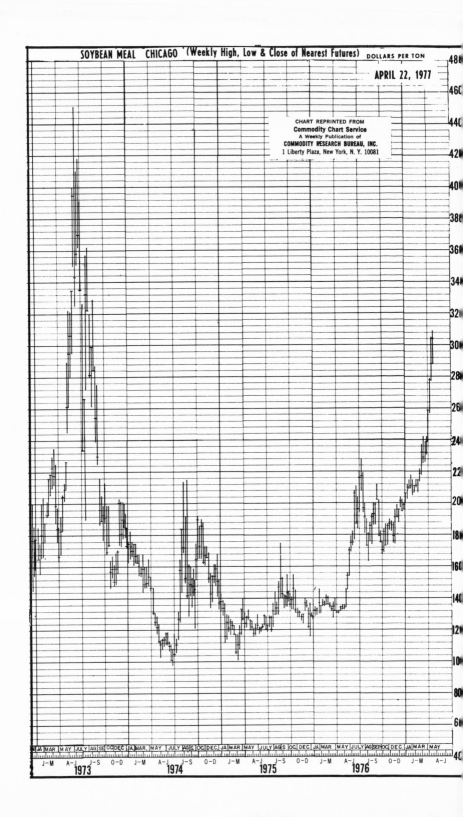

SOYBEAN MEAL CHICAGO (Weekly High, Low & Close of Nearest Futures) DOLLARS PER TON

APRIL 22, 1977

CHART REPRINTED FROM
Commodity Chart Service
A Weekly Publication of
COMMODITY RESEARCH BUREAU, INC.
1 Liberty Plaza, New York, N. Y. 10081

to them.

To figure the gross processing margin, you multiply the cash price of the meal by .025, the cash price of the oil by 11. Then, from the total of those two, subtract the cash price of the soybeans. The difference will be the gross processing margin.

For example, if cash meal is 80.00 per ton and oil is 10.80, the sum would be $3.18. If cash soybeans are selling for more than $2.92 per bushel, the processing margin is too small. Processors will then decide to cut back on their crushing operations. They will buy less soybeans and the price of soybeans will usually decline. If the cash price is low enough to give them 20¢ or more profit, they will be inclined to buy soybeans and the crushing will be increased.

Occasionally, as in November 1972, the price of Meal will sell at an unusually high price ($121 per ton) and Oil will sell at a depressed price (9.66). Soybeans sold at 3.67. This gave processors a favorable margin of 61¢ per bushel.

The above means that, if the price of meal and oil go up, soybeans will also tend to move up. If the prices of meal and oil sell off, soybeans should sell off.

On January 1st each year, there is a stocks in all positions report. This is important because it can help you estimate the potential supply and demand for soybeans until the harvest begins once again in September.

Soybeans need rain in July and August or the final crop may be smaller than previously estimated. That is somewhat bullish and the price of soybeans futures will remain at a higher level than would be the case if there was a more generous amount of rain.

During the harvest seasons, the elevator owners like to see the market close weak on Fridays. This helps them to buy beans at a lower price on Monday. Oil and meal exporters like to see a strong close on Friday so they can receive a better price when they sell on Monday.

SOYBEAN MEAL

Soybean meal is an economical, high-protein feed supplement that is used to feed hogs, cattle and poultry. The standard meal is 44% protein. Most of this meal is used in the United States, but exports to Europe, Japan and other countries are increasing.

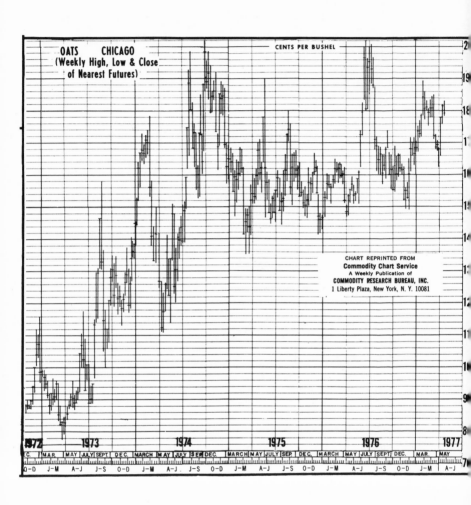

OATS CHICAGO
(Weekly High, Low & Close
of Nearest Futures)

CENTS PER BUSHEL

CHART REPRINTED FROM
Commodity Chart Service
A Weekly Publication of
COMMODITY RESEARCH BUREAU, INC.
1 Liberty Plaza, New York, N. Y. 10081

1972   1973   1974   1975   1976   1977

As farmers in those countries increase the number of cattle, hogs and poultry, they will need more of this high-protein supplement because it is an efficient and profitable source of feed.

A contract of soybean meal is 100 tons at 2,000 pounds (a total of 200,000 pounds) The minimum fluctuation is 5 cents per ton. A 1/8 cent fluctuation in the price of soybeans is just a bit larger than a 5 cent per ton fluctuation in meal.

It is difficult to store soybean meal for a long period of time so a crusher must find a market and move whatever meal he has produced. As long as the meal can be sold at a reasonable profit, crushing can be continued at a high rate. But crushers will not keep crushing soybeans if the large amount of soybeans crushed should cause the price of meal to decline— especially if it also causes the crushers to build stocks of unsold soybean oil.

When that situation occurs, the crushing rate must slow down. This causes less demand for soybeans. Soybeans will then sell off until the crushing margin improves. (See information on crushing margins under soybeans above.)

The demand for soybean meal is influenced by its price. If meal prices get too high, feed mixers will look for lower priced substitutes. This can cause a temporary increase in the supply of the meal and the prices will tend to move lower. And, if the supply of meal is small, the great demand for meal around the world will cause the prices of meal to rise.

The demand for meal is easier to estimate than the demand for oil because there are not as many protein meals to offer price competition for soybean meal. Fishmeal is the largest and most serious competitor as a high-quality protein feed. Other competitors are cottonseed meal, peanut meal and rapeseed meal.

To estimate the demand for soybean meal, you need to watch the numbers of cattle, hogs, poultry and sheep. If the total number is large, the demand for meal can be large. If there is an attempt to reduce the number of animals, or if the number of poultry is severely reduced, there may be less demand for meal in the coming months. An exception to that could be a large increase in the number of livestock and poultry in foreign countries. If those countries should have an increase, it would offset the smaller requirements in the United States.

SOYBEAN OIL

Soybean oil is an important commodity in both the domestic and international trade. Over 90% of the soybean oil produced is used as food in one form or another—salad dressing, margarine, cooking oil and, in the form of lecithin it is used in ice cream and candies. The other 10% is used in industry for many products ranging from plastics and paints to fuel additives.

More soybean oil is now consumed in human nutrition than butter and lard.

Soybean oil competes with olive oil, lard, tung oil, cottonseed oil, peanut oil, flaxseed oil, safflower oil, rapeseed oil, sunflower oil and sesame seed oil.

A contract of soybean oil is 60,000 pounds. Quotations are in points. 1 point equals 1/100 cents per pound. The profit or loss on 1 point is, therefore, $6 (100 points $600). A 1/8 cent fluctuation in soybeans is equivalent to approximately 1 point per pound for oil.

The price of soybean oil can be influenced by competition from other oils. If, for example, there is a large production of sunflower seed, prices of sunflower oil might decline and, temporarily, this could turn the attention of oil buyers away from soybean oil to sunflower seed oil. If there is a large production of hogs, lard will be plentiful and, if lard sells at a lower price, commercial bakers may use more lard for shortening. Also a large crop of peanuts, cotton, rapeseed or any other crop that produces oil or any combination of those crops, in any area of the world, can cause pressure on the price of soybean oil.

If soybeans move higher in price, but oil and meal prices do not move higher at the same time, processors say the crushing margin is not favorable. They will then cut back on their processing operations until the gross processing margin is more favorable. This will, temporarily, create less oil and could help to firm the price of oil. If, however, there is a substantial increase in the price of soybean oil, it will encourage the crushing of soybeans and, thereby, increase the supply of oil.

OATS

Oats are grown in most countries, but the heaviest production is in the United States and Canada, followed by Europe and Russia. The total world supply is approximately 3 billion bushels. The United States production is usually about 30% of the total world supply.

A bushel of oats weighs 32 pounds. A bushel of corn weighs approximately 56 pounds. Oats are used primarily for feed for livestock and poultry. They are also an unusually good feed for horses. (About 5% of the total production is used for human consumption.) When you forecast the price for oats, the total feed supply and demand situation must be considered—just as it is done for corn and soybean meal.

Oats are harvested in the summer and they tend to be at their lowest price when they are marketed, primarily, in August. But a large quantity of oats may still come into the market as late as October. Due to the hedging pressure, the seasonal low price for oats will, generally, occur after mid-August into October.

At the same time that corn is under pressure from the corn harvest, the pressure from the harvest of oats is being relieved and oats will tend to rise. The price difference between oats and corn will, therefore, tend to have a better price relationship as feed after the winter months are over.

RYE

Rye is basically a European crop. The total production, world-wide, is approximately 1.5 billion bushels. That is small compared to the other grains. The leading producers are Russia, West Germany, the United States, Argentina and Canada.

The major use in the United States is flour milling for bread and crackers and distilling for alcoholic beverages. The European countries, especially West Germany, are net importers of rye where it is used extensively in the production of bread.

Rye is planted in late September through early November. It lies dormant through the winter. Then harvest begins in May and runs through July.

Prices of rye tend to decline from around February 1st to May 31st. After July 1st, prices tend to move higher until around November 1st. Then, there may be a period from November 15th to February 1st when rye prices will be in a trading range near the high of the move. While rye is in that trading range, it offers less of a clear-cut opportunity for profit. It should then be left alone while you look for better "special situations".

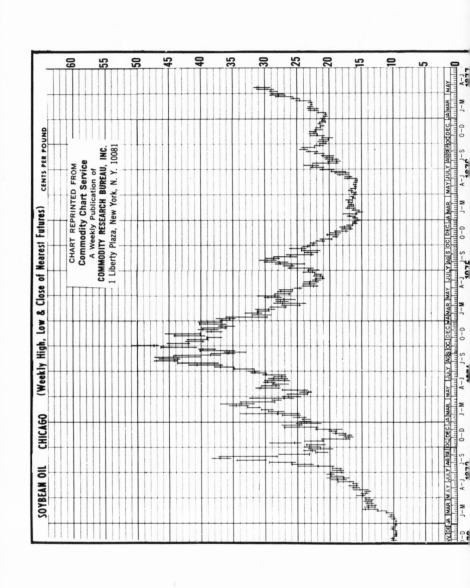

SOYBEAN OIL   CHICAGO   (Weekly High, Low & Close of Nearest Futures)   CENTS PER POUND

CHART REPRINTED FROM
Commodity Chart Service
A Weekly Publication of
COMMODITY RESEARCH BUREAU, INC.
1 Liberty Plaza, New York, N. Y. 10081

5

BASIC FACTS ABOUT MEAT AND EGGS

LIVE CATTLE

Live Cattle is the largest single commodity produced in American agriculture. Cash receipts from the marketing of cattle and calves in 1972 totaled more than $14 billion. That is more money than the amount received from the total sale of wheat, corn, soybeans and cotton combined.

Live Cattle are produced in every state, but the majority of cattle are raised in the Corn Belt and the large Western range states of Texas, Nebraska, Kansas, Wyoming, Montana, Colorado, Arizona, New Mexico and California.

The United States produces approximately 10% of the entire world population of Live Catttle. The next largest producers of cattle are in this order: Russia, Brazil, Argentina, Mexico, France, West Germany, Australia, Canada and the United Kingdom.

One contract of Live Cattle calls for 40,000 pounds of live animals which will usually average about 37 head.

Beef is considered the favorite food of Americans. From 1960 to 1972, the per-capita consumption of beef in the United States increased from 85 pounds per person per year to 116 pounds. Demand for beef depends on such factors as the size of the population, the economy and the prices of competing proteins such as poultry, lamb, pork, fish and cheese.

Whatever beef is produced is usually consumed quickly because there is a limited amount of storage space for beef. The price, therefore, will usually depend on the total supply of beef available at any time and, of course, prices of beef are always affected to some extent by other competing protein foods.

At times of high prices, the United States will import as much beef as possible from Argentina, Australia, Brazil, Ireland, Mexico and Canada. But there will be times when those countries will not have enough additional beef to export. At such times, prices will remain at a high level.

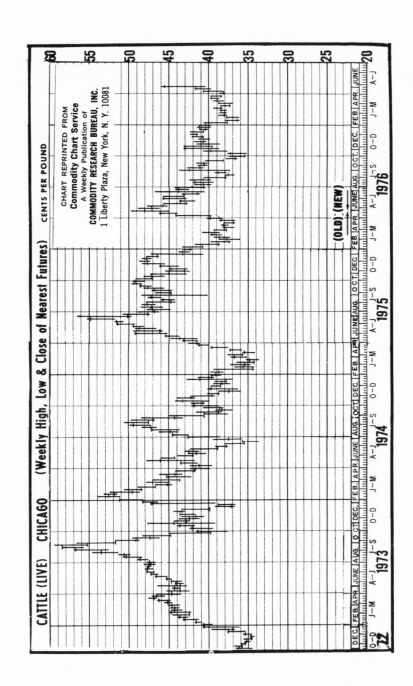

CATTLE (LIVE)   CHICAGO   (Weekly High, Low & Close of Nearest Futures)

CENTS PER POUND

CHART REPRINTED FROM
Commodity Chart Service
A Weekly Publication of
COMMODITY RESEARCH BUREAU, INC.
1 Liberty Plaza, New York, N. Y. 10081

(OLD)·(NEW)

1973   1974   1975   1976

THE CATTLE CYCLE

The production of Live Cattle follows a long-term cycle. One of the reasons is the lifespan of the cattle. It takes about two years to thirty months for a cow to grow heavy enough to bring to market.

If there is a severe drought in the cattle-raising states, there will be a smaller number of cattle available and prices to consumers will be much higher. Good grazing conditions and abundant feed supplies will encourage cattlemen to increase their herds.

Another factor that can affect the cattle cycle is the ratio of the price of cattle and the price of feed. This is similar to the facts concerning the hog-corn ratio given in Chapter 4 under CORN.

When the total number of cattle raised increases over the year previous, a larger number of new calves will mature. Slaughter will then increase because steers which have reached a marketable weight must be brought to market regardless of price at this stage of the cattle cycle. In other words, there is a time limit on how long cattle producers may withhold their cattle from the market. Eventually, they must be brought in because no one will buy a dead cow.

In years past, most cattle were sold direct to stockyards and many cattle continue to be sold in this way. But marketing is changing and an increasing number of cattle are sent to feedlots that specialize in raising cattle to maturity on specially prepared feeds that aim to give high quality beef. Then those cattle go directly from the feedlots to the packing plants.

As the marketing of cattle becomes heavier, prices begin to fall. The liquidation phase of the cattle cycle begins. Slaughter is then increased because herd exapnsion is no longer considered profitable. This can cause further pressure on prices. Finally, the total number of cattle becomes too small and prices begin to firm once again. At this point, the producers of cattle realize that a bottom has been reached. A new upcycle begins as an attempt is made to raise more cattle.

The decline in the cattle cycle may take a few years and the upward movement may also take a few years. An early indication of the buildup in cattle numbers occurs when producers withhold a large number of cows, calves and heifers from slaughter so they can rebuild their herds.

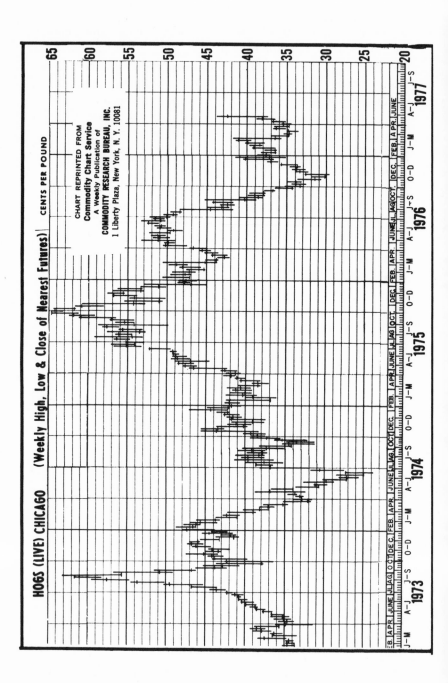

HOGS (LIVE) CHICAGO   (Weekly High, Low & Close of Nearest Futures)   CENTS PER POUND

CHART REPRINTED FROM
Commodity Chart Service
A Weekly Publication of
COMMODITY RESEARCH BUREAU, INC.
1 Liberty Plaza, New York, N. Y. 10081

Most calves are born between February 15th and April 1st. After about 26 months, a steer will weigh approximately 1,150 pounds and is ready for slaughter. The number of cattle ready for slaughter seems to be at its peak around September and October. Prices, therefore, are usually lower at that time. The smallest number of cattle are usually slaughtered in February and March.

LIVE HOGS

Trading in Live Hogs futures has had a steady increase in volume and open-interest since it was first introduced in 1966. In October 1972, the open-interest in Live Hogs had grown to a total of 19,500. That is 26% larger than the total open-interest of 14,500 in Pork Bellies at that same time.

The production of Live Hogs in the United States is concentrated in the Corn Belt area. The four states of Iowa, Illinois, Indiana and Missouri produce more than one-half the total U. S. hog production. Three other states, Minnesota, Nebraska and Ohio produce another 16%. The states of Georgia, North Carolina, Tennessee, Kansas and Kentucky have had a large increase in recent years due to the fact the production of hogs is now carried on in a more carefully planned way with better feeds.

The prices of Live Hogs and Pork Bellies tend to move along together. Much of this information concerning hogs, therefore, should be read if you trade in Pork Bellies. The extent of the moves for each one will vary. At times, one will go up while the other will go down and vice versa. If there is a large amount of bellies in storage, prices of belly futures will move up more slowly than hog prices. And, when there is a shortage of bellies in storage compared to the year previous, the price of pork bellies may rise much faster than the prices for hogs.

There is no storage supply of live hogs to weigh upon the market as there is in the case of bellies. During a time when marketings are small, live hog prices can move higher. But the price of Pork Bellies could decline if the storage stocks of bellies are, temporarily, larger than normal. Hog prices, therefore, can move up more easily if there is a smaller number of hogs coming to market compared to the previous week or the previous year.

Each Live Hog futures contract calls for 30,000 pounds of

Live Hogs. This means there are about 130 to 145 hogs marketed at an average weight of 200 to 240 pounds. No hogs under 190 pounds nor any over 240 pounds are deliverable on a futures contract.

A hog gains about 2 pounds per day until it weighs 75 pounds. 1.75 per day from 75 pounds to 125 and about 1.65 per day after 125 pounds. About 225 pounds of feed are needed to put on 100 pounds of weight. After 7 months a hog will reach the average slaughter weight of 220 pounds.

There are six terms you need to know concerning hogs. (1) Boars are male hogs used for breeding purposes. (2) Sows are female hogs which have given birth to a litter of pigs. These sows can usually be re-bred to produce another litter about 3½ months after the previous breeding. (3) A litter is approximately 7 pigs, but litters may run from 5 pigs to as many as 15. (4) Barrows are castrated male hogs. They produce better pork and gain weight faster than boars. (5) Gilts are young female hogs that have not yet given birth to a litter of pigs. (6) When a sow or a gilt gives birth to a litter of pigs, it is called "farrowing".

The largest number of pigs are generally farrowed during March, April and May. They are then marketed from August 1st to October 1st. The smallest number of pigs born usually occur between December and February. They are ready for market from May through June.

Hog prices tend to hit their low for the year from August through November. This is when the largest number of hogs come to market. Slaughter is also higher at this time of the year.

Prices of hogs, therefore, tend to be the highest during June and July when hog slaughter is at its lowest level of the year.

During a period of high hog prices, farmers will generally increase the size of their breeding stock and retain more gilts (the young female hogs). And, during a period of low hog prices, farmers will generally keep less gilts. A reduction in the breeding stock will then occur. This means that 6 to 8 months later, less hogs will be coming to market. Prices of hogs and belly futures, therefore, tend to rise.

When the Chicago wholesale price of bacon is over the 42¢ level, there will usually be a reduction in the consumption of bacon—up to 10% or more. Prices below 23¢ will often result in an increase in consumption. These consumption figures tend to increase after January until the summer months when they usually reach a peak.

Belly prices, therefore, are generally lower during the months of September through December due to the large supply on hand. And they are usually higher during the summer months of June through July when production is low.

High prices for hogs one year will stimulate over-production during the next year or two. This high level of production will then cause prices to decline. This tends to cause a decrease in the size of the next few pig crops. The slaughter rate will then decrease and the price of hogs will usually rise.

The hog-corn ratio discussed under CORN in Chapter 4 can help to show the direction in which hog production may be heading over the next six months—either up or down. When the hog-corn ratio is higher than normal (from 25 to 28) it is **more profitable for farmers to feed corn to hogs. And, farmers will also try to increase their herds and feed more hogs. When the hog-corn ratio is low, around 12 - 15, farmers prefer to sell their corn and market their hogs at lower weights.**

Either a change in corn prices or a change in hog prices can cause a change in the hog-corn ratio.

When prices of hogs are low and starting to move up, farmers will usually increase the size of their hog production. When prices are falling, they may reduce the size of their breeding herd.

The cost of feed makes up about three quarters of the cost of producing a hog for market so the cost of feed will affect the total production costs and cause farmers to plan to either increase or decrease the total number of hogs on their farms.

When feed prices are low, hog producers tend to feed hogs to heavier weights. This can lead, later, to lower prices. When feed prices are high, hogs tend to be marketed sooner at lighter weights.

THE HOG CYCLE

You can estimate hog prices in the future when you understand the hog cycle. The normal cycle averages about four years in length. It is normally divided into two stages. From a peak, prices move down to a lower level. Then there is a move up to a point below that peak. Then a move down to a point below the previous low. From that low point, which is approximately two years from the peak price, prices will then

PORK BELLIES   CHICAGO   (Weekly High, Low & Close of Nearest Futures)   CENTS PER POUND

CHART REPRINTED FROM
Commodity Chart Service
A Weekly Publication of
COMMODITY RESEARCH BUREAU, INC.
1 Liberty Plaza, New York, N. Y. 10081

105
100
95
90
85
80
75
70
65
60
55
50
45
40
35
30
25
20
15

BRUARY MR MAY JULY F E B R U A R Y MR MAY JULY AG F E B R U A R Y MR MAY JULY AG F E B R U ARY MR MAY JULY AG F E B R U A R Y MR MAY

-D   J-M   A-J   J-S   O-D   J-M   A-J   J-S   O-D   J-M   A-J   J-S   O-D   J-M   A-J   J-S   O-D   J-M   A-J
72   1973   1974   1975   1976

move up to a higher level. Prices will then decline to a low above the previous low. The following year, prices will usually move back towards the previous peak made four years earlier. Whether prices will exceed that peak or fall short will depend on many factors such as inflation of the economy, demand for pork, ham and bacon, actual supply and projected plans by farmers for the months ahead.

The primary substitutes and competition in the market are beef, poultry and fish. If the price of these other protein sources go up, people will tend to eat more pork, ham and bacon. And, if the prices of beef, poultry and fish go down, it can cause prices of pork, ham and bacon to mover lower also.

The demand for bacon, hams and pork tend to reach their peak during the summer and fall months. This is due to the large number of people who take vacations during July, August and September and they tend to eat more luncheon meats and bacon rather than beef.

The demand for pork and bacon tends to be lowest during January through April. Ham consumption increases during Thanksgiving and Christmas, also at Easter time.

Bad weather such as ice, snow, heavy rains, floods, below zero temperatures or excessively hot temperatures cause hog producers to bring less hogs to market. Prices, therefore, tend to rise a little at such times.

PORK BELLIES

Pork Bellies (the underside of the hog) is known by the public as bacon. This futures market, for many years, has been one of the best potential money-makers of any commodity both on the bull side and the bear side. The margin is reasonable, the leverage is good and the profits are larger— if you are right.

The Pork Belly contract calls for frozen, unsliced slabs of bacon with an average weight of 12 to 14 pounds in carload lots of 36,000 pounds. The two bellies cut from each hog will average about 10% of the hog's weight. Bacon production, therefore, can usually be estimated by taking 10% of the total weight of hogs slaughtered.

To determine the supply outlook for Pork Bellies, you must analyze the hog situation. Read the section on Hogs. Pigs are farrowed (born) all year long and they are raised until they reach commercial weight between the 5th and 8th months. At that time, the hogs are ready for slaughter.

To estimate whether the hogs will be slaughtered during their 5th month or near the end of the 8th month, you need to look at the hog-corn ratio. (Most any of the better commodity brokers can get that figure for you.)

A low hog-corn ratio (12 -16) means that when the price of corn is high in relation to hog prices, farmers will prefer to sell their corn at those higher prices and market their hogs at an earlier time—usually 5 to 6 months. A high-corn ratio 24 - 28 (as occurred in 1972) means that the price of corn is low in relation to hog prices. Farmers will then feed more corn to their hogs and market those hogs at a later time when they are are 7 and 8 months old.

If hogs are slaughtered early, the average weight of slaughtered hogs will be low. The opposite is true if the hogs are kept until they are nearly 8 months old.

In every year, there is a seasonal pattern of prices that can help you buy futures contracts at low prices and sell them at higher prices later on. The reason is—the spring pig crop (the pigs born between December and May) will account for 55% to 60% of the total hog production for each year.

Pork Belly prices are strongly influenced by the increase or decrease of hog production. The total number of hogs available for slaughter will usually reach a peak during the months of October to January. Belly production will increase at this time. This will cause storage stocks to increase. Supplies, therefore, will usually exceed the demand. This will cause the price of Pork Bellies to reach their low between late September and late December. Slaughter then declines until a low point is reached sometime between June and August. This is when the storage stocks are usually the smallest and the price of futures will generally make a top during one of those months.

Although that seasonal price pattern occurs quite regularly each year, there are factors that can cause a variation in that pattern. The most important factors that affect Pork Belly prices are:

1. The size of the pig crop.
2. Monthly and weekly cold-storage figures.
3. Weekly bacon slicings.
4. Daily, weekly and monthly slaughter.

5. Farrowing intentions by farmers.
6. Hog-corn price ratios.
7. Average weight of hogs slaughtered.

BULLISH INFLUENCES ARE

1. Smaller than expected arrivals at the 11 markets.
2. Smaller receipts at those 11 markets than the previous week or the previous year.
3. Less hogs delivered in Iowa-Minnesota than expected.
4. Higher cash hog prices.
5. An increase in the price of cash bellies.
6. Daily hog slaughter less than the previous week and previous year.
7. Bacon slicings somewhat larger than the previous week's report. (Published after the close on Friday.)
8. The total out of town storage movement more than a year ago. (Published after the close on Tuesday.)

The more of those 8 bullish factors you have in any one day or during any 5 day week, the more bullish the trend will be.

BEARISH INFLUENCES ARE

1. Larger than estimated hog arrivals at the 11 markets.
2. Larger receipts than the previous week or the previous year.
3. Larger than expected receipts in Iowa-Minnesota markets.
4. Lower cash hog prices at most of the 11 markets.
5. A decline in the price of cash bellies.
6. Daily hog slaughter larger than the previous week and previous year.
7. Bacon slicings (issued after the close on Friday) somewhat smaller than the previous week and the previous year.
8. The out of town storage movement (issued after the close on Tuesday) less than a year ago.

The more of those 8 bearish factors you have in any one day or during any 5 day week, the more bearish the trend will be.

FOUR YEAR CYCLES IN BELLY PRICES

Past statistics indicate there is a four year cycle in the number of hogs and pigs on farms beginning January 1st each year. At the same time, there has also been a four year cycle in belly prices.

When the number of hogs goes from a large supply to a smaller supply, it tends to cause prices to rise from a cyclical low to a cyclical high. This usually takes about two years.

Then, as the production of hogs begins to increase due to those high prices, belly prices will decline in price over a period of approximately two years from that top to a new bottom.

Through 1975, the years when low prices have been made are 1956, 1960, 1964, 1968, 1971, 1974. The highs have been—1953, 1957, 1961, 1965, 1969, 1973, 1974 and 1975.

During each two year up-move and each two year decline, the long-term trend will be interrupted by sharp seasonal countermoves. The swing in prices from high to low then back to high (over a four year period) will vary with certain important factors. They will be influenced by the increases or decreases in the size of the hog production, the size of the slaughter and the amount of frozen bellies in storage.

During the years beginning January 1, 1952 - 1956 - 1960 - 1968 - 1972, the number of hogs on farms were at or near the maximum production. Farrowing intentions, however, pointed to a reduction in the coming pig crops. Prices were then at a cyclical low. A strong seasonal rise began in the winter months that lasted into the summer months. Then a seasonal decline occurred. (In 1952 and again in 1964, prices declined all the way back to the lows made at the beginning of the year. In 1956 and 1960, the decline was not as steep.)

During the years 1953 - 1957 - 1961 - 1965, the number of hogs on farms beginning January 1st were down from the year before. The market had a strong bull move from the winter lows up to the summer highs.

When the shift in production of hogs is large compared to the year previous as it was in 1953 and 1965, there is a tendency for the market to recover quickly from the seasonal break.

CASH PRICES IN RELATION TO FUTURES

The spread between the futures price and the cash price will come closer together as the near month approaches the time when it must go off the board.

As a general rule, the best time to buy Pork Bellies is between October and January when the market is usually at a seasonal low. The July delivery gives you a considerable amount of time to take advantage of the seasonal advance. In 15 out of the last 19 years, (1953 - 1972), the cash market made a low between October and December. In the other four years, the low was made no later than the following May.

In 15 out of the past 18 years, the high was made sometime between early July and early September. In two of those years, the high was made in April. In 1965, the high was made in December.

If the cash price moves up during the months between March and July, the futures will, generally, move up also. But the cash price should move up a bit faster than the futures. If the cash price lags behind the futures and the futures sell at a big premium over the cash, the commercial interests who deal in the cash will find that high premium is an excellent spot to "hedge". This can stop the rise in futures. Eventually, the weight of the hedge selling by those commercial interests plus the liquidation by disappointed longs can break the market. Once prices start down, the decline can increase at a rapid rate. That is what happened on May 17th, 1972 when the market broke over 700 points (7¢) in three weeks.

No matter how good the fundamentals may appear for several months—in the future, there is always a possibility of a decline in price when the supply of bacon in storage is still **large and the prices of May and July futures are too high in** relation to the cash. That fact is especially true if those high prices occur, prematurely, in the first year of the two year upcycle.

A bullish or bearish cold storage report can be anticipated to some degree by watching the daily and weekly storage figures from Chicago and the out-of-town warehouses. From that information, you can get an idea of how many pounds of Pork Bellies were stored or taken out of storage during the previous month.

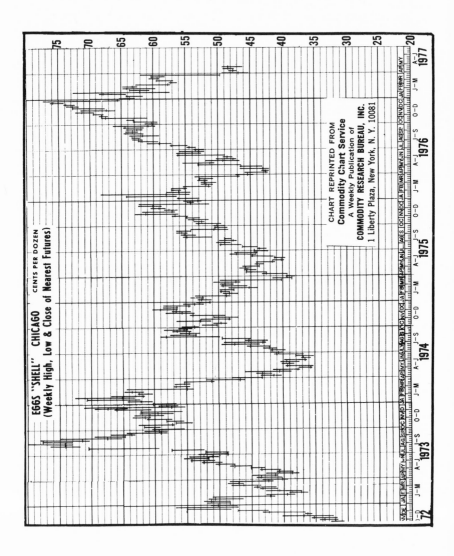

EGGS "SHELL" CHICAGO CENTS PER DOZEN
(Weekly High, Low & Close of Nearest Futures)

CHART REPRINTED FROM
Commodity Chart Service
A Weekly Publication of
COMMODITY RESEARCH BUREAU, INC.
1 Liberty Plaza, New York, N. Y. 10081

The quarterly pig crop report, issued around December 22nd, March 22nd, June 22nd and September 22nd often creates large and sudden moves after its release. This report gives the amount of hogs and pigs on the farms on the 1st of the month the report is issued. It also indicates the number of hogs and sows according to weight, the farrowings during the past 6 months and the intentions to farrow during the coming 6 months.

The number of hogs on farms together with the actual far-rowing during the past 6 months will give you an idea of the number of hogs that may be marketed during the 6 months after the report. That, together with the number of hogs farmers intend to farrow have important long-term significance.

You can anticipate the way the market might move after these reports by taking into account the hog-corn ratio for the previous six months and the possible ratio for the coming six months. If the hog-corn ratio might be high, prices of futures may be high. If the hog-corn ratio might go lower, less corn will be fed to hogs than in previous months. Hogs will then come to market earlier (around 5 to 6 months old) and at lighter weights.

After May, the movement of bellies into storage usually becomes less. From June through August, it is necessary to find ways to sell those bellies in storage. The price of cash bellies may then sell over the price of the futures. The premium will depend on the amount of bellies in storage. If there is a large amount of bellies in storage, the futures might be 2¢ to 3¢ under the cash market. And, with a smaller number of bellies in storage, the cash price might sell only ½¢ to 1c over the futures.

EGGS

Eggs are one of the least expensive sources of protein. The United States is the world's largest producer of eggs. Production is more than 60 billion eggs with an average income of more than $2 billion. The U.S.S.R. is the next largest producer with approximately 30 billion.

Shell eggs are traded in carload lots of 22,500 dozen. The minimum price fluctuation is 5/100¢ per dozen (5 points)— $11.25 per contract.

To estimate the future price of eggs, you should try to determine the basic supply-demand factors. This depends on an estimate of egg production, the distribution of the various grades of eggs and the supply-demand factors during any given delivery month. The production of eggs will usually affect the retail price and, to some degree, the amount of consumption. Several factors affect the supply of eggs. They are (1) the number of actual layers, (2) the average output for each layer and (3) the storage stocks. The first two factors are the most important.

Feed is the largest item of expense for poultry raisers. The egg-feed ratio is the number of pounds of feed equal in value to one dozen eggs. If this ratio is low, feeding is more expensive. A higher egg-feed ratio indicates that feed is cheap. High feed costs will encourage poultry raisers to reduce their flocks and cut down on feed. This is why statistics on culling will usually be contrary to the trend in cash egg prices. Low feed prices will encourage those poultry raisers to order more new chicks from the hatcheries.

The demand for storage eggs cannot be accurately estimated. Quite often, therefore, storage eggs will sell at a discount to the fresh eggs. That is why most of the shell eggs stored today are hedged. These eggs are usually readily available to offset the lower amount of production in the fall and winter. This helps to reduce the shortage of fresh eggs at that time. During the spring, fresh eggs are produced in large quantities. This tends to depress the cash egg prices. Shell eggs placed in storage between February 1st and July 31st may be used for delivery against the September contracts. Eggs placed in storage after July 31st are not eligible for delivery.

When the price of egg futures sells above the cost of storing eggs, it is profitable for the egg dealers to store and sell the futures. This hedge helps to protect the storer against a price decline. After the storage period (July 31st), September futures should sell 3 cents or more below the price of fresh eggs. If storage stocks are large, the futures price will usually reflect whatever grade of eggs is the lowest priced. And, at such times, the futures price may sell as much as 10 cents below the wholesale cash price quoted on the New York City market.

6

BASIC FACTS ABOUT
THE INTERNATIONAL COMMODITIES

London is the commodities capital of Europe. This is where most of the action is in the European markets.

More than 460 million people live within 600 miles of London. That is more than double the 230 million of both the the United States and Canada. This large population area is, therefore, an important force for the consumption of commodities. As more people in Europe become aware of commodity futures as a trading medium, there will be a tremendous surge of interest in London commodities. When this comes, London commodities may trade in a volume as large as the volume of trading in the United States.

There are fewer futures markets in London than in the United States, but there is active trading in Cocoa, Sugar, Silver, Coffee, Rubber, Tin, Copper and Wool. Other futures contracts that may become more active in the future are Soybean Oil and Sunflowerseed Oil.

On a comparison basis, in February 1972, the open-interest in Cocoa in London was 35,000 tons of 5 tons per contract against 10,000 contracts of 15 tons each in New York. In Sugar, the London and the New York markets were about equal. In Coffee, London had 10,000 contracts open while New York had only 7. The London mid-day quote for Copper is used as a basis for fixing prices of Copper throughout the world.

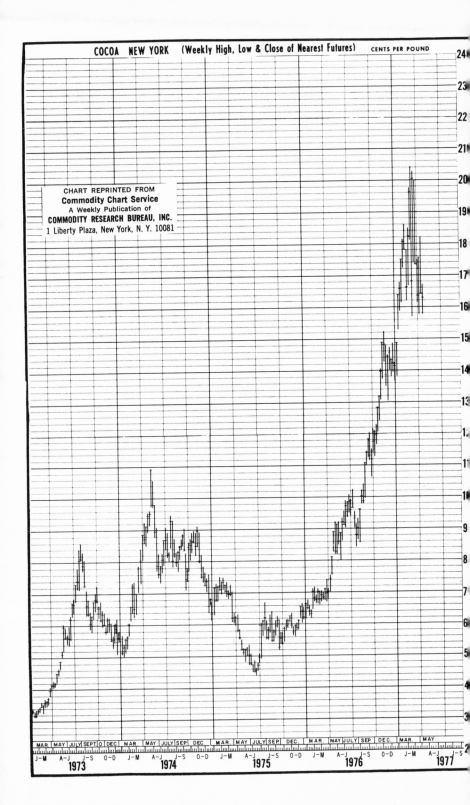

COCOA NEW YORK (Weekly High, Low & Close of Nearest Futures) CENTS PER POUND

CHART REPRINTED FROM
Commodity Chart Service
A Weekly Publication of
COMMODITY RESEARCH BUREAU, INC.
1 Liberty Plaza, New York, N. Y. 10081

1973   1974   1975   1976   1977

COCOA

Trading in Cocoa is done, primarily, on the London Cocoa Terminal Market and the New York Cocoa Exchange. It is a favorite commodity for professional traders who like to trade for longer periods rather than short-term because Cocoa tends to move over a wide price range and, once the direction—up or down—is established, that direction tends to continue and is relatively difficult to reverse.

Due to the fact the London market opens five hours before the New York market, traders in the United States can often gauge the possible trend in Cocoa prices by watching the price action of Cocoa on the London market before the New York market opens each day. And, of course, traders in London may use the action of the New York market to gauge their decisions concerning whether to buy or sell Cocoa in London the morning after the New York market closes.

The six largest producers of Cocoa are Ghana, Nigeria, Ivory Coast, Cameroons and Togo in West Africa and Brazil in South America. Trees are now being planted in Malaysia and that area may sometime in the near future become a substantial producer of Cocoa. The West African countries, at the present time, produce about 76% of the world's Cocoa. But, as Brazil and Malaysia increase their production, that percentage may slowly decrease.

It takes about five years for a Cocoa tree to bear fruit and mature. Two crops are produced each year. Weather conditions can affect the total production. Excessive rains can wash away many of the cocoa pod flowers off the trees. If the weather is too dry, the flowers may dry up and fall off the trees.

The crop year in Cocoa runs from October to March for the main crop and from May to June for the smaller mid-crop. In Brazil, however, the mid-crop has been larger than the main crop. About 80% of the total world output is harvested from late September through March and only about 20% from April through August.

Ghana is usually the first country to release an estimate of the main crop. That report will usually be given out near the last week in September. Nigeria will usually report a week or two later. Because these two countries are large producers of Cocoa, their reports are watched very closely to gain an estimate of the potential size of the total crop world-wide.

The supply of Cocoa is determined by the stocks on hand on October 1st plus the potential production. Demand for Cocoa comes from cocoa and chocolate manufacturers who "grind" the cocoa beans to make their products. The larger the "grindings", the greater the use and demand. The smaller the "grindings", the smaller the use and demand.

Cocoa prices tend to follow a seasonal pattern. While such a pattern is not definite, prices tend to move down after the heavy main crop shipments from late November until March or April. As the needs of the manufacturers are filled, demand tends to pick up in July and August in anticipation of heavy fall grindings. Most of the crop has been sold out by that time. Only the harvest of the mid-crop in Brazil offers any pressure against the market.

During the months of July and August, crop scares may occur. By the middle of November, however, a more accurate estimate of the final crop may be made. And, if prices have risen rapidly until that time, a sharp decline may occur— especially if there should be a large amount of hedging from manufacturers around the world. Pressure may then increase until around February or March. If, however, there should be a shortage of Cocoa, the market could move up instead of down, during those same months.

A high point in Cocoa prices will often occur early in October. If prices in November, however, are higher than in October, it means that demand is, temporarily, greater than the supply and prices may continue to move higher until early in January.

The producers in the four major African countries try to time their sales to a percentage of the anticipated total crop production. Once the producers have sold their crop, the hedging pressure eases off and the market can then move up once again.

One factor that can cause Cocoa prices to decline occurs when the Finance Minister of one of the African countries tells the Marketing Company to sell Cocoa no matter what the market price may be so he can obtain foreign exchange. This can create a downward move in the futures market even though the fundamentals do not justify that action.

Information on grindings is made available on a quarterly basis by the leading Western consuming countries (the

U.S.A., West Germany, United Kingdom and the Netherlands) which consume about 45% of the annual world crop.
Grinding figures from the Soviet Union and other countries
are not published regularly.

The above factors create a situation where the fundamentals are less reliable than in some other commodities. Professional traders, therefore, who are good "chart readers" and
know how to act upon the basis of their charts can make
large profits trading in Cocoa.

Grindings in the countries that produce the Cocoa have
been increasing. They now amount to about 15% of the
world's total.

World production of cocoa and chocolate products can increase because nearly two thirds of the world's 4 billion population have never tasted cocoa or chocolate. When a market is
created to serve those billions of people, cocoa production and
the sales of cocoa should increase.

Cocoa manufacturers rely on whatever information they
can gather from the producing countries. Then, after they
estimate the total world production and consumption, they
will plan their purchases for the coming season. If a large crop
is forecast, they may decide to wait until the following year
to cover most of their commitments hoping, thereby, to
secure their cocoa at lower prices. If, however, there may be
a shorter crop than normal, they may enter the market early
and buy as much as possible before prices move too high.

SUGAR

There are two types of sugar. Sugar cane and sugar beet.
Sugar cane is grown in tropical and sub-tropical areas. The
United States grows both cane and beet sugar. The growing
season for cane may be from 12 months in Florida and
Louisiana to as long as two years in Hawaii. Sugar beets are
generally planted in the spring and harvested in the fall. Due
to the large demand and consumption, the United States
needs to import from 4.2 million to 6 million tons of sugar
each year.

Sugar is planted and harvested somewhere in the world
every month. Europe and Russia produce beet sugar. Planting is in the spring and harvest occurs during October through
November. The U.S.S.R. is the world's largest sugar producer.

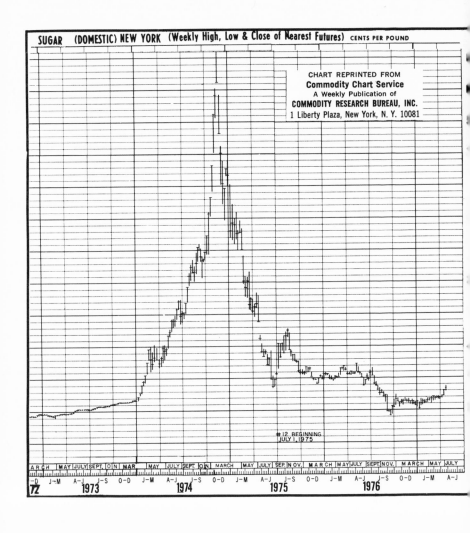

SUGAR (DOMESTIC) NEW YORK (Weekly High, Low & Close of Nearest Futures) CENTS PER POUND

12. BEGINNING
JULY 1, 1975

ARCH |MAY JULY|SEPT.|O|N| MAR |MAY |JULY|SEPT |O|N| MARCH |MAY |JULY |SEP.|NOV. | M A R CH |MAY|JULY SEPT|NOV. | M A R CH |MAY |JULY

-D J→M A-J J-S O-D J-M A-J J-S O-D J-M A-J J-S O-D J-M A-J J-S O-D J-M A-J
72 **1973** **1974** **1975** **1976**

Brazil is second, Cuba, third and India, fourth.

Too much rain at harvest time may reduce the yield. Once the cane matures, it must be harvested without delay to assure the best yield. 20 tons per acre is considered a good yield. If the sugar content averages 14%, 2.8 tons of finished raw sugar will be harvested. Sugar beets will average about 12 tons per acre with an average of 15% sugar to produce about 1.8 tons of raw sugar per acre. The harvested cane and sugar beets must then be processed and refined to make the raw sugar.

Cuba is the largest exporter of sugar. When the crop is normal, Cuba will account for 20%-30% of the world's exports. The Cuban crop is cane. It is harvested during the winter and spring months. Heavy rains and hurricanes can cause damage to the Cuban crop and decrease the final size of the crop.

Two-thirds of the world's sugar is controlled by import quotas, export quotas, preferential markets, guaranteed prices and other trade requirements. The other one-third is "free sugar". It is known as "world sugar".

There are two contracts. The #10 contract is domestic sugar. The #11 contract is the world sugar contract and this is the best contract for trading. The #11 contract calls for 112,000 pounds of sugar. Prices are quoted in cents. 1 point (1/100¢ per pound) is $11.20. World sugar is traded in London at the United Terminal Sugar Market and in New York at the New York Coffee and Sugar Exchange.

World sugar stocks are the important influence on prices. An increase in those stocks on September 1st (the beginning of the season) indicates that supplies are large enough to offset the demand. A reduction in the supply of world sugar can lead to an increase in price. Total stocks of sugar are determined by stocks on hand September 1st plus the potential production of sugar world-wide.

Consumption increases with the increase in the population which can increase the demand at an average rate of about 3% per year. On the demand side, the United States, Russia, Great Britain and Japan are the largest buyers. Economic prosperity also helps to increase the use of sugar. A decline in prosperity, of course, can cause the total consumption to decrease.

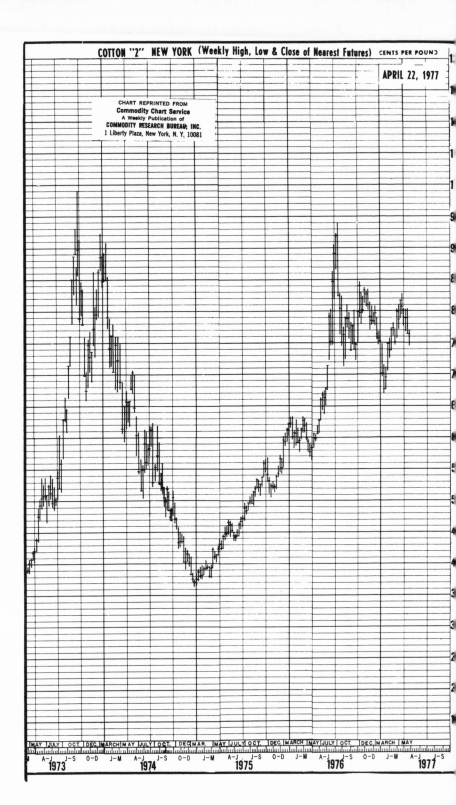

COTTON "2" NEW YORK (Weekly High, Low & Close of Nearest Futures) CENTS PER POUND

APRIL 22, 1977

CHART REPRINTED FROM
Commodity Chart Service
A Weekly Publication of
COMMODITY RESEARCH BUREAU, INC.
1 Liberty Plaza, New York, N. Y., 10081

Sugar produced from sugar beets is the same quality and has the same final use as sugar produced from cane. A high percentage of beet sugar is raised in Europe and the production in those countries has a great influence on the price of world sugar. If production in the European countries is short, prices will rise rapidly as they did early in 1972 and, again in the fall of 1972. If production of European sugar beets is heavy, however, prices will decline.

A possible substitute for sugar may come from the conversion of dextrose to fructose. This can produce a new corn-based liquid sweetener that may, in the future, offer serious competition to the present dominance of sugar as a sweetener.

SEASONAL PRICE MOVEMENTS

Prices of sugar have no definite seasonal price pattern. But large moves—both up and down—can be followed by observing the figures for open-interest and volume.

SOURCES OF INFORMATION

New York Coffee and Sugar Exchange Weekly Review. This review contains daily information on futures trading as well as the latest domestic statistics.

U.S.D.A. Sugar Reports. Issued monthly by the Department of Agriculture. It gives market reviews, world statistics and the United States statistics on sugar.

F.O. Licht's International Sugar Report. (Published by F. O. Licht, K.G. 2418 Ratseburg, Schleswig-Holstein, West Germany). This is a highly respected report that covers the daily and bi-monthly estimates and statistics relating to sugar.

COTTON

Cotton is an important fiber grown in many areas of the world. It grows best in countries that have hot weather with adequate occasional periods of rain.

There are four major production areas in the United States. (1) The South Central area—Mississippi, Arkansas, Tennessee, Louisiana and Southeastern Missouri produces more than 30% of the cotton grown in the United States. Most of the planting in this area is done in April and May then harvested from late September until mid-November. (2) The Southwest —Texas and Oklahoma produce about 30% of the total U. S. production. Planting begins in early March in the Rio Grande Valley and is harvested during July and August. In the high plains area of West Texas and Oklahoma the planting and harvest occur about one month later . (3) California, Arizona and New Mexico produce about 20% of the crop. Most of this cotton is grown on irrigated land. This results in a high yield per acre and a high-qualty, long staple variety of cotton. (4) The Southeast—Georgia, Alabama and the Carolinas produce less than 15% of the crop. Most of the planting in this area is completed by the end of April and is harvested from October to early November.

A futures contract in Cotton consists of 100 bales (50,000 pounds) of cotton. Price is quoted in cents per pound. Minimum fluctuation is 1/100¢ per pound—$5 per contract.

Cotton's use as a textile has decreased in recent years due to the greater use of man-made fibers. But the large increase in the population, world-wide, tends to outweigh that loss. This, in time, will create some gains in total mill consumption.

A report on planting intentions and acreage allottments issued in March will give you an early indication of the potential production. The actual figures for planted acreage are issued in July and December.

Weather developments can affect the quantity and the quality of cotton. Too little rain tends to slow down plant growth. Too much rain can cause late maturity. Rains and cold weather early in the season can delay planting. If that should cause cotton to be late, an early frost can injure the cotton and reduce the final yield. Wet and cool weather in September and October can result in boll rot. In the summer months, boll weevils and bollworms may attack the crop, but they can usually be controlled by poisoning if heavy rains do not wash the poison off the plants.

Figures on "mill consumption," released monthly by the Census Bureau, concern the actual consumption of raw cotton. Figures for "domestic consumption" are the total consumption of cotton in finished goods and is the total of mill consumption plus the raw cotton equivalent of imported textiles minus the raw cotton equivalent of exported textiles.

SOURCES OF INFORMATION

The Cotton Situation Report issued by the U. S. D. A. Economic Research Service in January, March, May, July, September and October summarizes data and includes an assessment of the cotton market.

SILVER

Silver is one of the world's most precious metals. It is produced in almost every country in the world. The largest producers are Mexico, the United States, Canada and Peru. Those four countries produce approximately 60% of the world's silver. Russia and Australia are the next largest producers.

Production of silver has consistently fallen short of total consumption. Mines of silver are now nearly depleted. The major portion of silver is now recovered as a by-product from the treatment of other base metals such as copper, lead, zinc and tin. Demand for the price of those less-precious metals will, therefore, have a large affect on the total production of silver. If those metals decline in price, or less amounts should be mined, silver then becomes short and the price of silver available should go up.

Billions of dollars of silver are now hoarded or kept in the form of antiques, silverware, jewelry and religious items. And, throughout Europe, the Middle East, India and other countries, many banks and wealthy individuals have millions of ounces of silver, in one form or another. If the price of silver should rise high enough, some of that hoarded silver might then be sold or melted down. Sea water is another potential source of silver if ways can be found to get it out of the ocean.

Silver is prized for its brilliance, resistance to rust, excellent electrical properties and other advantages that make it a valuable metal, world-wide, for coins, jewelry, religious ornaments and a growing number of industrial uses.

Industrial demand for silver is increasing. The largest use is for photographic film, plates and sensitized paper. Scientists are continually working on ways to use a substitute for silver in film or reduce its content. To economize on its use of silver, the photographic industry has learned to extract silver from their photographic solutions. If a substitute for silver can be found for photographic film, it could, temporarily, cause the price of silver to decline.

The second largest user of silver is the electrical and electronics industry. As an electrical conducter, silver has proved to be efficient and dependable for switches, relays and components in computers and in telephone and aviation equip-

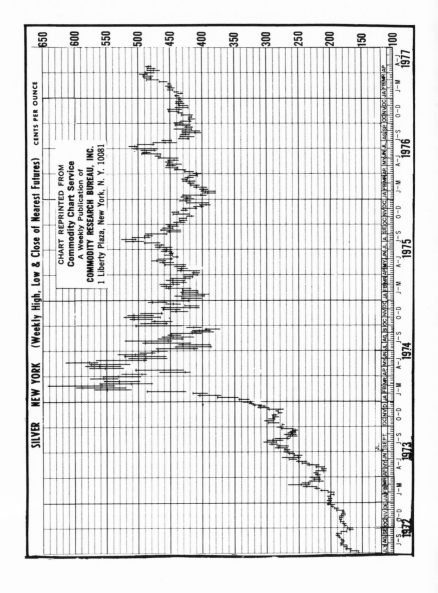

SILVER NEW YORK (Weekly High, Low & Close of Nearest Futures) CENTS PER OUNCE

CHART REPRINTED FROM
Commodity Chart Service
A Weekly Publication of
COMMODITY RESEARCH BUREAU, INC.
1 Liberty Plaza, New York, N. Y. 10081

ment. The silverware and jewelry industry is the third largest user of silver.

Large profits can be made from trading in silver futures because the price of silver will, oftentimes, move rapidly in relation to the actual supply and demand.

A silver contract calls for 10,000 troy ounces of silver refined to .999 fineness or higher in bars cast in weights of 2,000 ounces each.

COPPER

Copper is a volatile and often times profitable commodity in which to trade. A move of only 4¢ gives a profit or loss of 100%. The price of copper futures will, often, fall sharply when the total world supplies begin to increase. And, when the world stocks of copper are at their lowest level, prices of copper will sell, once again, at high prices.

Copper is produced in many areas of the world. The major producers are the United States and Canada. The next six largest producers are Russia, Zambia, Chile, Peru, the Congo and the Phillipines.

Copper enjoys widespread consumption in industry because it has excellent electrical and heat conductivity, resistance to corrosion, malleability, strength and ductility. And it can be readily alloyed with both nickel and silver.

Consumption of copper has shown a steady long-term growth pattern. As an important material for use in industry, the price of copper is closely tied with the state of the economy. It is wise, therefore, to look to the prospects for the future of business in all the large industrialized nations that use large amounts of copper.

A·contract of Copper calls for 25,000 pounds. A 1¢ move (100 points) results in a profit or loss of $250. Margin is usually $1,000 and commission is $36.50.

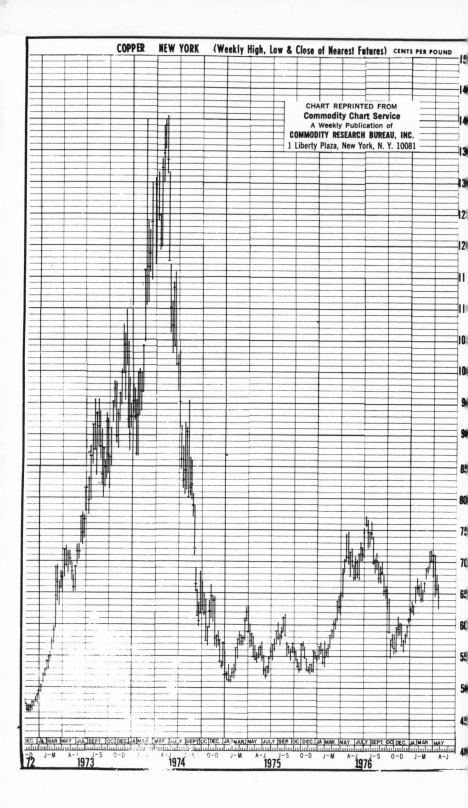

COPPER NEW YORK (Weekly High, Low & Close of Nearest Futures) CENTS PER POUND

CHART REPRINTED FROM
Commodity Chart Service
A Weekly Publication of
COMMODITY RESEARCH BUREAU, INC.
1 Liberty Plaza, New York, N. Y. 10081

7

BASIC FACTS ABOUT OTHER COMMODITIES

This chapter contains information on five commodities that have varied levels of importance. Some, like potatoes, are decreasing in importance. Others, particularly the financial futures, are now the most traded of all the markets. Sometime in the near future, they may be added to the

Other commodities are being considered for futures trading. Some time in the near future, they may be added to the present list of 20 major commodities. They will be designed, like the stock index futures, primarily for the benefit of commercial interests.

FROZEN CONCENTRATED ORANGE JUICE

In 1972, over 25% of the world's production of oranges were produced in Florida. Florida also produced about 75% of the total United States production. California produced 20% and the remaining 5% were grown in Texas and Arizona. Florida production in 1970-71 was 147.3 million boxes of 90 pounds each compared with 58.5 million boxes in 1949-50.

Oranges are a weather sensitive crop. They can be hurt by cold and sudden heat. Every year, they must survive the hurricane season during September and October, also the freeze period which lasts from November until March. Sudden heat waves can cause young fruit to fall off the trees. Hurricanes and strong winds may cause large numbers of fruit to fall and decrease the size of the crop.

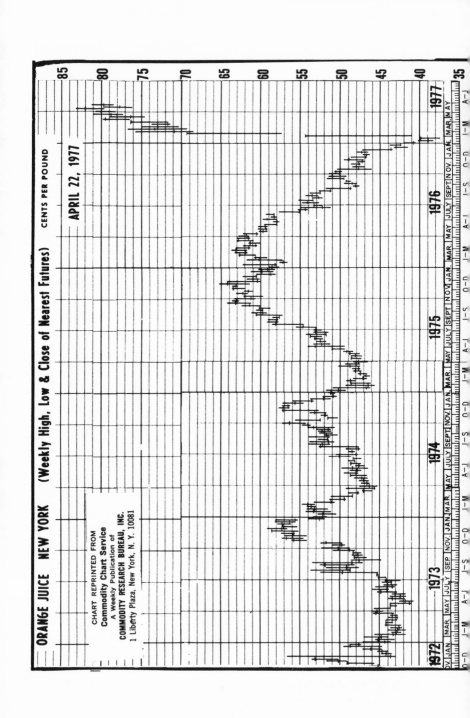

ORANGE JUICE NEW YORK (Weekly High, Low & Close of Nearest Futures) CENTS PER POUND

APRIL 22, 1977

CHART REPRINTED FROM
Commodity Chart Service
A Weekly Publication of
COMMODITY RESEARCH BUREAU, INC.
1 Liberty Plaza, New York, N. Y. 10081

Oranges are usually picked from December until June and early July. The harvest of mid-season and navel varieties (about 50% of the total crop) ends around March 1st. The other 50% consists of Valencia oranges which have a higher juice content and a sweeter flavor.

The larger the crop of oranges, the lower the price may be. And, of course, a smaller crop will generally cause the price of futures to rise. Carryover is also important. Low year-end supplies in July can cause an increase in price and a large carryover can cause prices to sell at a lower level.

To help orange growers, processors, packers, wholesalers and super-markets secure a smoother and more profitable market, a futures contract was developed for frozen concentrated orange juice. This contract is quoted in terms of 55 gallon drums of 15,000 pounds each with an average of 3% orange pulp. The value of a 1¢ move (100 points) is $150.

Wholesale grocers, supermarkets and institutional distributors find the Florida Concentrated Orange Juice futures market an excellent place to "hedge" one of their important sales items because it can be merchandised in the same form that they buy it. They can place "buying hedges" and use their long positions to protect a low price. Then they can plan promotions of frozen orange juice when prices are higher. This allows them the opportunity to acquire large amounts of orange juice at low prices while, at the same time, there is no need to tie up large amounts of money in warehouse space or lay out a large sum of money in actual inventory.

The continued upward trend in the use of Florida Concentrated Orange Juice is due to both an increase in the per capita consumption and the expanding population. Worldwide, there is a possibility that production may be larger than the demand over the next few years. The United States is the leading exporter. Canada is the number one buyer. Other major buyers are the United Kingdom, West Germany, Sweden, the Netherlands, Switzerland and Belgium.

In spite of the large production in the United States, imports of Frozen Concentrated Orange Juice into the United States have been increasing. To date, the amount of imports have not exceeded 2½% of the total U.S. production so those imports have had little influence on prices in the United States.

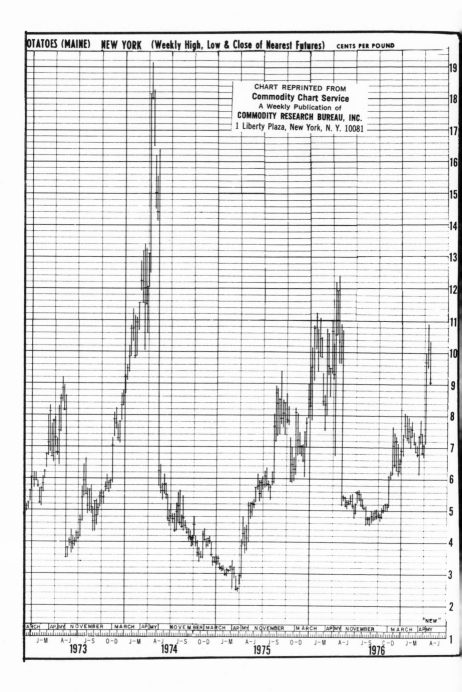

OTATOES (MAINE)   NEW YORK   (Weekly High, Low & Close of Nearest Futures)   CENTS PER POUND

CHART REPRINTED FROM
Commodity Chart Service
A Weekly Publication of
COMMODITY RESEARCH BUREAU, INC.
1 Liberty Plaza, New York, N. Y. 10081

Brazil, the second largest exporter is now becoming a major competitor for the United States in the world market. The climate in Brazil is a bit more favorable than in Florida. **There is also a larger amount of land available to plant more** trees. Production and sales from Brazil may, therefore, continue to increase. The total number of trees in Brazil increased from 13.6 million in 1960 to more than 48 million in 1972. This compares with 56 million orange bearing trees in Florida in 1973. The next largest country to consider for imports is Israel.

To estimate potential supply, the most important figures to watch are the U. S. D. A. crop and yield estimates which are given out about the 10th of each month from October through July. The weekly figures compiled by the Florida Canners Association are issued every Wednesday after the market closed. They indicate the total movement for the previous week from processors into wholesale grocers, supermarkets, institutional distributors and manufacturers who use some Frozen Concentrated Orange Juice in their products.

The reports above however, are only estimates of final production. You must always take into consideration the possibility that a severe freeze, hurricanes, too much rain or an unusual period of drought can effect the final production.

As a general rule, the price of FCOJ futures tends to move up from the middle of October to the end of January. During this **freeze scare period, growers and processors are** usually reluctant to place selling hedges for their crops because their crops might be damaged during that period. If that were to **happen, prices could move higher and they would lose money** on their premature "short hedges". Professional traders know this so they help prices move higher—provided there is, obviously, no severe threat to the crop. Then, at the end of January, prices tend to move lower as the growers and processors become less concerned about the freeze damage. At this time, they will then place some "short hedges" to protect themselves against a possible decline in prices during the harvest season. Those short hedges, of course, add some pressure to the market.

MAINE POTATOES

Potatoes are harvested in some area of the United States

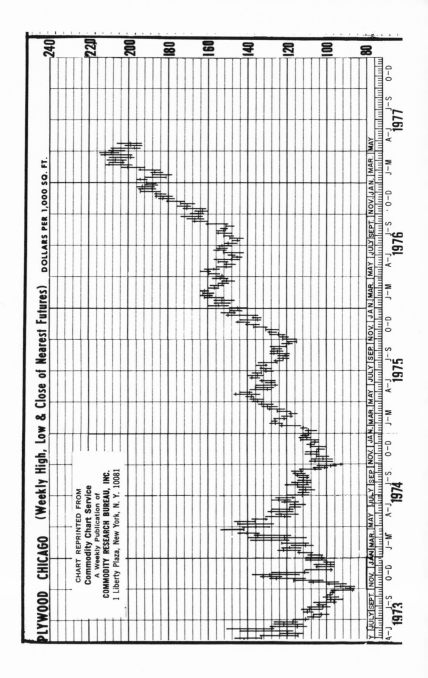

PLYWOOD CHICAGO (Weekly High, Low & Close of Nearest Futures) DOLLARS PER 1,000 SQ. FT.

CHART REPRINTED FROM
Commodity Chart Service
A Weekly Publication of
COMMODITY RESEARCH BUREAU, INC.
1 Liberty Plaza, New York, N. Y. 10081

almost every month throughout the year. Most of the production, however, is concentrated in the areas of Aroostook County, Maine; Kern County, California; the Red River area of North Dakota and Minnesota; the Snake River area in Idaho; Long Island and some areas of Florida and South Carolina. These areas have accounted for 80% of the total U. S. production of potatoes. Harvest in those areas occur from August through October.

The Maine Potato contract is designed to help the growers reduce their risk and give them an opportunity to establish a price for their crop months in advance. It also helps the wholesalers and processors fix their raw material costs **so they can more easily make firm commitments on orders for the future.**

With potatoes sold through a futures contract, a potato **farmer knows what he will receive. He protects the price of** his crop through a "hedge" on the futures market. When he sells his crop on the cash market, he will buy back his hedge. In this way, the grower has reduced the risk of loss from a decline in price.

The potato shipper can offer his customers potatoes for future delivery at a firm price over or under the hedged month. The shipper can then permit the buyer to fix the time of final sale at a later date. This protects the shipper's profit and gives him greater flexibility in his purchases and sales.

When a potato processor thinks the current futures price is advantageous, he will buy a futures contract to build up his inventories. This makes it possible for that processor to carry an inventory without the large investment of storage, interest and insurance necessary if he actually owned the potatoes. Later, when he buys the actual potatoes, he will sell his futures contract. If he feels that potato prices may decline, he will sell a future contract to protect himself against the possible loss. As he makes sales of his cash potatoes, he will then buy back his hedge in the futures market to offset the amount of cash potatoes that were sold.

A contract of potatoes is 50,000 pounds of Maine grown potatoes, packed in 50 pound burlap bags. They must meet United States standards in effect on the day of delivery. Price fluctuations are in 1/100 cents per pound—$5.00 per contract. A 1 cent (100 points) move is $500.

PLYWOOD

Plywood is a versatile and widely used building material. Extreme and rapid price movements have often occurred due to weather conditions, labor relations, demand for housing, interest rates, and a wide variety of other factors that have all helped to cause the sharp rises and declines in price. This makes plywood a difficult commodity for the average trader who is not able to secure enough facts nor understand the fundamentals that cause such rapid changes in price. Only an experienced chart reader who is an agile trader should ever trade in Plywood.

A contract of Plywood is one boxcar loaded with 36 banded units—69,120 square feet per car. Prices are quoted in minimum fluctuations of 10 cents. A 1¢ move is 69.12.

LUMBER

22% of the total land area of the United States is made up of commercial forest. The lumber production is concentrated in two areas—the Southeastern United States and the Pacific Northwestern states of Washington, Oregon and Northern California.

The major demand for lumber comes from residential construction, some commercial construction, remodeling and other uses such as furniture, manufactured products, mobile homes, etc. The use of lumber depends on the seasonal influence of the construction industry, especially residential building. Production, therefore, is generally lowest during December and January and highest during late summer and early fall. In addition, lumber often has a problem with substitutes such as metal studs and plywood. Plastics are also being used in such areas as shutters, millwork and furniture.

Those conditions cause dynamic changes in the price of lumber and the futures market tries to reflect those changes. It offers a good medium for protection for the commercial interests who must deal in lumber, but this commodity is risky and difficult for a trader who is a speculator and tries to guess which way the lumber market might move in the near future. Generally speaking, the only way a speculator should trade in lumber futures is at a price level which is near a low point reached in a previous year or at a high point reached a year or two earlier.

MONEY MARKETS AND FINANCIAL INSTRUMENTS

In recent years, the various commodity exchanges have added a number of trading mediums such as Gold, Treasury Bills, Treasury Bonds, Ginnie Mae's, foreign currencies and S. and P.'s (Standard and Poor's Averages).

These trading mediums are not truly commodity markets in the same sense that Corn, Wheat, Soybeans, Copper, Cotton, Live Cattle, Sugar, etc. are. They are more risky and their price movements are difficult to estimate because they are, too often, caused by decisions made by governments and those decisions can oftentimes be somewhat sudden and unpredictable. With margins of 10% or less, losses in these markets can be severe.

No one knows what the governments of various countries, like Russia, South Africa, the Arabian countries, China and others, might do with their stocks of gold and their decisions are usually based on what is in their best interest. In the United States, decisions by the Federal Reserve can also be sudden and unpredictable.

These are volatile markets and large losses as well as large profits can occur. The reason is news and rumors about such factors as interest rates, inflation, devaluation, revaluation, shifting trade balance in world markets and a combination of other factors.

Every trader likes to talk about the large profits he made, but he is reluctant to talk about the times when he took large losses in the "money markets"—especially if those losses were large ones.

It is a common belief among traders outside the Commodity Exchanges that floor traders have many advantages. They say to themselves, "If I were only a floor trader, I could do better and make more money."

But consider this true story reported on the business page of the Chicago Sun-Times (November 12, 1982). This story told how a 10 year veteran trader lost $850,000 in only a few weeks. A fellow trader described him as a nice quiet little conservative trader.

He explained his loss with these words, "The market went against me. I do not sit on a big position. I am small compared to some of the bigger traders. But the most difficult thing in futures trading is the ability to close out a losing position. If you don't have that, you end up like I did."

"The bond market is a big, vicious, fast market and I got caught in a big swing. It was no small loss, but the $850,000 is much smaller than some of the others who do not get this amount of publicity."

And many so-called sophisticated investors are unable to escape disaster. Consider the $1 billion, 700 millions of assets of the Greater New York Savings Bank. This bank took a loss of $40 million early in 1980 on trades in their Ginnie Mae's. And these were in the actual Ginnie Mae's, not the more risky futures.

PLATINUM

Platinum is a white, precious metal that is growing rapidly in importance in many phases of industry. It is valuable because it can take a high permanent polish, can withstand high temperatures, oxidation and stress. Due to its unique properties, platinum can be used in such fields as jewelry and chemicals for the production of nitric acid, fertilizers, explosives and plastics. In the electrical industry, it is used for thermo-couples, precision instruments and control devices. In the glass industry, it is used to manufacture fiberglass. But the largest user of platinum is the petroleum industry. And a new potential use for platinum is as a catalyst for catalytic converters to control pollution.

The use of platinum may continue to increase if the growth of the industries above should also increase. The only problem lies in the world-wide state of the economy. So long as business is good, large amounts of platinum will be used. If the economy should slow down, the industrial use of platinum may also slow down.

The U. S. S. R. is the largest producer of platinum. South Africa is a close second. Canada a distant third. The United States is the largest consumer. Consumption in Western Europe and Japan, however, should soon increase at a rapid rate.

The price of platinum futures depends on the forces of supply and demand as well as the changes in the various currencies around the world.

A contract of platinum calls for 50 troy ounces. A 1¢ move is $50.

8

THE IMPORTANCE OF VOLUME
AND OPEN-INTEREST

Open-interest refers to the total number of new purchases and sales made each day. When a seller sells a contract to a buyer, his interest in the contract is "open" until he closes out his interest with a buy order. And the buyer's interest in that contract is also "open" until he closes out his contract with a sell order. The total open-interest, therefore, is—1 contract—because the buy order and the sell order are opposite sides of the same contract.

At the end of each trading day, the total number of long contracts are balanced out with an equal number of short contracts. This total is known as "the open interest".

The volume of trading is also considered as—1 contract—for the same reason.

The total size of the open-interest indicates the amount of interest in that commodity. It is also an important factor when you want to determine the liquidity of the market in any commodity.

As long as the open-interest in a commodity and the daily trading volume are both large enough, they will provide a market liquid enough to trade. Generally, both the volume and the open-interest will be large enough in Wheat, Corn, Soybeans, Pork Bellies, Live Cattle, Cotton, Cocoa, Sugar, Silver, Live Hogs and Copper.

Occasionally, you will find both the open interest and the volume large enough in Eggs, Potatoes, Plywood, Lumber,

Iced Broilers and Oats. There is also a possibility that three of those commodities—Plywood, Lumber and Iced Broilers will, eventually, show a much larger open-interest than their totals in 1972.

An increase or a decrease in the open-interest helps you to know whether traders in a commodity are willing to follow prices higher or lower. This is shown in an increasing amount of interest in that commodity as prices move up or down.

In grains, the open-interest is expressed in millions of bushels. In other contracts, the open-interest is stated in the total number of contracts. For example, an open-interest of 300,000,000 bushels of Corn at a value of $1.50 per bushel indicates that the total interest in Corn has a value of $450,000,000. And an open-interest of 36,000 contracts in Live Beef Cattle (40,000 pounds for each contract) at 40 cents is $560,000,000. The open-interest in Live Cattle is larger than in Corn because Live Cattle is the largest single commodity produced by farmers in the United States.

To help you understand the importance of changes in open-interest, consider the following figures. An increase of 5,000,000 bushels in the open-interest of Corn indicates an increase of $7,500,000 at $1.50 per bushel. An increase of only 5,000 contracts of Live Cattle may create an increase of $80,000,000. That is more than ten times as large as Corn.

Open-interest in any trading month always begins at a small figure, close to zero. As more and more traders and commercial interests become interested in trading that month, the open-interest will increase. As the time for expiration of that month draws near, open-interest will fall off until its final day when, once again, it will be close to zero.

Because each month goes from zero to a larger figure back to zero, you cannot gauge the trend of the market accurately enough by keeping open-interest figures on only one month. You will get a more accurate indication of the strength or weakness of a move if you use the total open-interest figures only.

Most of the news services give the total open-interest figures every day. Those total figures can help you gauge the impact on the market that an increase or decrease in that total can bring.

The open-interest will increase only when new orders to buy are matched by new orders to sell. If a trader is long one or more contracts in the morning, then sells out sometime before the close, there is no change in the total open-interest because one order cancels out the interest of the other. The volume figures, however, would increase by the number of trades closed out. And, many times, traders will buy and sell several times during one day. This can create a large amount of volume with little or no actual change in the open-interest.

For a strong bull move to continue, it needs many new traders who are willing to buy at higher prices. Sellers, generally, will tend to sell less eagerly than they do in periods when prices are in a congestion or in a declining market. This lessened desire to sell creates less pressure on the market and buyers who need to buy will continually raise their bids until their buy orders are filled.

These bids to buy come from three sources:

1. Speculative buyers who believe if they buy today, prices may be higher in a few more days.

2. Traders who were short and want to buy back those shorts before they lose more money due to higher prices—and

3. Commercial interests who are generally short. They will buy back those short hedges as they successfully market their cash products.

For a strong bear move to continue, the reverse is true. It needs more traders who are willing to sell at lower prices. Buyers, generally, will be less willing to buy. This lessened desire to buy plus a greater desire to sell creates more pressure on the market and prices move towards lower levels.

You will get a more accurate feel of the effect of volume and open-interest if you will—

1. Keep a chart of weekly (high-low-last) price changes.

2. Add up the volume of sales for each trading day. Then divide that total number of sales during the week by 5 (or 4 if one day during the week was a holiday). This will give you an average volume of sales for that week. Draw vertical lines between the weekly average figure.

3. Use the total open-interest figures for either Monday or Friday (choose one or the other) and draw a connecting line from one week's figures to the next. This will result in a somewhat wavy line as that open-interest grows larger or decreases.

4. Now look at the changes. Compare them on a long-range basis. Is the open-interest line moving up or down? Is the trading volume larger or smaller than several weeks ago?

Open-interest cannot increase, in an uptrend or a down-trend, unless new buyers or sellers replace those traders who are "stopped out".

WHAT THE TOTAL OPEN INTEREST MEANS WHEN IT INCREASES

IF PRICES GO UP — and the open-interest increases — this is technically strong and shows that some shorts are being "stopped out", but new short sellers are taking their place. Those who are bullish and want to be long are more aggressive and continue to buy. This combination of higher prices and an increase in the open-interest, indicates that higher prices should follow.

IF PRICES CHANGE VERY LITTLE — and the open-interest increases — it indicates a "trading market". Those who want to go short are selling to those who want to go long. No definite trend is given and, usually, it is wise to stand aside and not trade in that market. (Wait for a better indication. It will come and you will then feel more certain you are right.)

IF PRICES GO DOWN — and the open-interest increases —it indicates that some longs are getting out, but new buyers are coming in. The large commercial interests are "hedging" and more traders are selling short. This is technically weak and lower prices should soon follow.

WHAT THE TOTAL OPEN INTEREST MEANS WHEN IT GROWS SMALLER

IF PRICES GO UP — and the open-interest grows smaller — it indicates that shorts are covering (getting out of the market). This is technically weak and, after the top has been completed, prices should decline.

IF PRICES GO DOWN — and the open-interest grows smaller — it indicates that those who were long are selling out. This is technically weak. Short sales at this time can help to depress the market. This will be shown a few days later when the open-interest increases as prices fall.

WHAT THE TOTAL OPEN INTEREST MEANS WHEN PRICES CHANGE VERY LITTLE

WHEN PRICES CHANGE VERY LITTLE and the open interest grows smaller — it indicates that the bulls are selling to the bears. Or, it may be only a "trading market". No definite trend, therefore, is shown. This is a time when you should stay out of that commodity for a few days or a few weeks. Wait for a better indication or look for a "special situation" in some other commodity. (See Chapter 9)

WHAT THE TOTAL OPEN INTEREST MEANS WHEN THAT TOTAL CHANGES VERY LITTLE

IF PRICES GO UP — it indicates the bulls are buying and the shorts are covering. This often occurs during rallies in a bear market or during an indecisive "trading market". It is not a time when you can trade safely. There is no strength indicated for the bulls. And there is no pressure indicated for the benefit of those who want to go short. It is wise, therefore, to wait for better clues in that commodity or look for a "special situation" in another commodity.

VOLUME ALSO HAS A MEANING

In addition to the open-interest, the volume of trading also has a meaning.

1. In a bull market, the volume of sales should increase as prices rise. If the volume does not increase, it may be a false move or "a trap". Even though your charts may show a "breakout" towards higher levels, the upmove should never be trusted unless it occurs with an increase in the volume of sales.

2. Volume of sales should be less on days when prices decline. If sales are considerably less on down days than on up days, this is bullish because it indicates that traders are not anxious to sell. (Many of the sales on these down days

will come from commercial interests who have to sell in the futures market to protect their cash business.) See the information on "hedging" in Chapter 3.

3. In a bear market, the volume of sales should increase as prices decline.

4. The volume of sales, in a bear market, should be less on days when prices rally. If the sales are considerably less on the up days than on the down days, this is bearish because it indicates that very few traders want to buy. (Many of the buy orders on those up days will come from commercial interests who buy back their short hedges because they have sold their commodities for cash and, therefore, no longer need the insurance they had from their "short hedge").

5. Near the top of a bull market, the volume of sales tends to slow down. Then, for one or two days, some news story or rumor may cause a dramatic rise. Shorts try to cover in a hurry. And some shorts who had gone short prematurely are forced to buy back their shorts because they were called for more margin. Those two factors cause the market to "blow off". Then, on the day when there are no more scared shorts left to buy at the higher prices, the market will turn down and close lower. On the day this buying climax comes, you will find it has made its high on a large volume of trades.

6. Near the bottom of a bear market, the volume of sales is usually small. There seems to be very little interest in that commodity. Some news or rumor, however, may cause a "selling climax." Weak longs are forced out near the bottom. The market then turns around. A new bull market will then begin to form.

9

SPECIAL SITUATIONS
THE KEY TO LARGER PROFITS

From a practical standpoint, it is good business to trade only in "special situations". In fact, special situations are the key to larger profits. This means you should avoid all inactive commodities.

Why waste your time in an inactive commodity? If you are not certain which way a commodity might move, it is best to stay out of the market. You can always lose if you are wrong. So do not trade until you, first, look through your charts and find a commodity in which you believe a "special situation" is developing. There are four reasons why:

1. Special situations are opportunities in which your potential for profit should be at least 60% or more in a few weeks.

2. You are less likely to make a mistake and wind up with a loss.

3. The profits come faster after a move gets underway.

4. You save a considerable amount of time. Instead of riding up and down in a trading market, you are more likely to see the market move in a dependable direction — the way you want it to go — either up or down.

A "special situation" occurs when the open-interest, trading volume, the fundamentals and your reading of the charts all indicate that prices should move far enough to earn a profit of at least 60% (after commissions) on the margin required.

So look for "special situations". Quite often, this means you should turn your attention away from certain commodities that you may, personally, like — especially when they are in an indefinite "trading range" — and begin to trade in a commodity that looks like it may be getting ready to move much faster in a definite direction.

If you subscribe to the Commodity Trend Service (see chapter 15) and you carefully study the charts of the 20 major commodities, you will find that one or more "special situations" will occur every month. These special situations offer you opportunities for profit that are much better than in other commodities where the picture is not quite so clear.

You must allow enough time to pass for the charts to develop one of the buy or sell patterns given in Chapters 12 and 13. And, from those patterns, you will find one or more situations where there is a possibility you can earn at least 60% or more on your investment after you enter your trade.

This means that, after you find a "special situation," you must buy or sell only when you believe that fundamentals will pull the market—up or down—in the direction you want it to go. Charts can help you because they make it easier to time your order to buy or sell.

The "moving averages" explained in Chapter 11 will also help you. If you keep an accurate record of the "moving averages", they can save you much time and help you select more of those "special situations". Your profits, therefore, should be much larger.

Your analysis of your charts should also point out places to put your stop-losses so that, if prices do not move in the direction you anticipate, your loss will be comparatively small. In other words, you should feel that the potentital profit you see in a "special situation" is at least three times as large as the possible loss.

If you aim to always look for special situations that can give you that 3 to 1 possibility you can be certain that, over a period of one year, you should be able to earn 360% or more on your money.

This means you must look for the minimum gains listed for each of the commodities below and the maximum amount of loss per trade is given at the right.

Commodity	Minimum amount of potential profit	Maximum loss 20% per trade
	(Amounts required include commissions)	
Broilers (Iced)	82 points	37 points
Cattle (Live)	70 points	10 points
Cocoa (New York)	170 points	30 points
Copper (New York)	254 points	65 points
Corn	6½ cents	1¾ cents
Cotton (New York)	150 points	49 points
Eggs	160 points	27 points
Hogs (Live)	71 points	15 points
Lumber	340 points	55 points
Oats	4¼ cents	⅜ cent
Orange Juice	430 points	100 points
Plywood	470 points	185 points
Pork Bellies	140 points	55 points
Potatoes (Maine)	44 points	18 points
Silver (New York)	645 points	155 points
Soybeans	12½ cents	3½ cents
Soybean Meal	330 points	67 points
Soybean Oil	55 points	15 points
Sugar	58 points	22 points
Wheat	7¾ cents	3 cents

Make certain that—if prices move sharply against you—put in an order to close out your trade before the close. Why **suffer a larger loss the following day? Take your small loss.** Then stay out of that commodity for at least two more days. If you decide to buy or sell, you will find your judgment is better on the third day and, if the time then is right, the market is more likely to move in your favor.

You need the potential profit of 60% given beside each of the above 20 commodities so that your earnings will be large enough to offset any losses you may have. Then, at the end of each month, you should be able to wind up that month with a net gain of 30% or more. And, of course, if you do not earn at least 60% on most of your trades and you find you must take some losses occasionally, you will never earn an average of 30% per month.

The ability to know which commodity to buy or sell and what time to buy or sell is the reason why the better traders can make a lot of money in commodities. They have learned to look for and trade, primarily, in "special situations". This means they never continue to trade in the same commodity week after week and month after month as if that commodity were the only one to consider.

Professionals in the stock market explain that fact with these words, "Don't marry a stock". They, too, look for "special situations".

For example, many people bought General Motors in 1964 between 105 and 114. Nine years later their trade still showed a loss as prices moved below $35 per share. Another great favorite in 1964 was American Telephone and Telegraph. It looked good to those who bought when it traded between 70 and 74. But, eight years later, in 1972, they could buy it for less than $45.

At the same time those two favorite stocks were going down, other less popular stocks moved up for gains of 100% or more.

This need to look for and trade in "special situations" is the primary reason for this book. If certain commodities are inclined not to move, look for those that do. In fact, this is the only sensible and logical way you can *build a fortune in commodities.*

Now you can see why it is necessary to move from one commodity to another as "special situations" develop.

If you do your own work and know how to select a good "special situation", you may do as well as some of the advisory services. The advisory services, however, will charge you as little as $2.00 to $4.00 per week (tax deductible) for their time and efforts.

It is obvious that you could never employ any individual to spend as much time on detail and analysis as an advisory service must spend for the low fee of only $2.00 to $4.00 per week.

Another advantage of an advisory service is — you can use that service to "double check" your decision to buy or sell a certain commodity. Such an advisory service may agree with your selection or it may disagree. In either case, it can often give you a new point of view and help you to finalize your judgment.

All of the older and larger advisory services have many hundreds of subscribers. Quite often the combined number of trades made by those hundreds of subscribers can help to move the market dramatically if the advisory service should be right in its conclusions.

10

RULES YOU SHOULD FOLLOW FOR SUCCESS

"Everybody loves a winner", they say. And you can win if you will follow the rules. But, if you do not follow the rules, you will never be a professional. Eventually, you will be a loser. How many people will love you then—only you will know.

Read and re-read these rules over and over again till they become second nature. Then you will have the feel and the know-how necessary to help you *build a fortune in commodities.*

If you should ever lose money on a trade—there is a good reason why you lost. Go back and read these rules once again. You will find that one or more of these rules were ignored. Ask yourself why you ignored that rule. Then try to correct your trading habits.

All professionals do this and you should, too.

RULE 1

HAVE A DEFINITE PLAN AND STICK WITH IT

You must determine two things: (1) At the end of each trading day, you must take the time to analyze the action of the market, consider the fundamentals, then plan what you will do the next day—buy, sell, hold or stand aside.

(2) Before the opening of the market each day, you must double-check your analysis of the night before. Something new may have occurred. If you understand the fundamentals and you still believe the market may move in your favor—up or down—then act upon that analysis. Once you act, and put your plan to work, you can change and correct your course as you go.

RULE 2

LOOK FOR SPECIAL SITUATIONS

Avoid all inactive commodities. Small profits will never help you *build a fortune*. Why waste your time and tie up your money in an inactive commodity? Instead, look for commodities that offer you an opportunity to gain at least 60% or more in only a few weeks. Quite often, this means you must turn your attention away from certain commodities you may, personally, like — especially those that are in an indefinite trading area — and trade in a commodity that looks like it may be getting ready to move much faster in a definite direction.

RULE. 3

THE PRICE OF EVERY COMMODITY WILL MOVE UP OR DOWN BEFORE THE FUNDAMENTALS ARE GENERALLY KNOWN

This is an important rule to learn because, until you learn this fact, you will, in the majority of cases, lose more money than you win.

In brief, this rule means that, when prices are high, they prove the fundamentals are bullish—*at that time*. And, when prices are low, they prove the fundamentals are bearish—*at that time*.

To determine where prices might go during the next few weeks or months, you must try to analyze what the fundamentals might be—*in the future*.

That is the important point to consider. See the chart on page 38 in Chapter 2.

After prices have been at a high level for several weeks, they will soon move down towards a point where sometime in the future, the fundamentals will be more bearish than bullish.

When the fundamentals and the news are bearish, they will prove that low prices in the market are justified. Prices will then make a base. Soon they will move up to a higher level where the fundamentals and the news will, once again, justify the higher price.

When you understand this rule, you will realize why so many professional traders say, "The market will often discount the news and move in the opposite direction."

RULE 4

CONTROL YOUR EMOTIONS

The biggest weakness of every individual (no matter who he may be) is giving way to wrong emotions. The emotions that can cause you to lose the largest amount of money are— fear, greed, lack of courage, hesitancy, "hope", a desire to gamble and inability to blame yourself for mistakes.

Other emotions that have always proved to be costly are— over enthusiasm at the top of the market and "panic"—if things do not go right.

When you learn to control those emotions and trade according to the rules in this book, you will not complain nor criticize someone else if you lose. You will also find it easier to trade with logic and reason.

Successful traders know they will suffer a loss from time to time. But they never hold on stubbornly to a losing position. They try to keep their losses small. They take their loss. Then they try to do better the next time.

RULE 5

WHEN YOU MAKE A MISTAKE—ADMIT IT

It is important to realize that you will make mistakes. Prepare yourself for them. Try not to expect your decision to buy or sell will be perfect. Every professional—no matter what activity he may be engaged in—will make an error in judgment or fumble the ball.

Disappointments will occur. But, whenever you make a mistake, you should admit it readily and as quickly as possible. A hard-headed, stubborn attitude can cost you more money. If you fail to admit a mistake or "hide your head in the sand", the mistake will not go away.

Many traders refuse to take a loss because they believe their "paper loss" is not a loss at all.

The truth is—wise investing always requires you to be realistic. Whether your loss exists on paper or you actually take your loss, in either case, it is real. The greatest mistake is to close your mind and pretend such a loss does not exist.

If you keep your mind calm, every loss you take should help you become a better trader. In time, you will learn what to do. Then you will find that, each time you trade, you will make fewer mistakes. And the more you learn from those mistakes, the more professional you will become.

RULE 6

DETERMINE THE TREND — UP OR DOWN THEN FOLLOW IT

The small orders you place have little effect on the market. The large commercial companies, interested in each commodity (see chapter 3 concerning "Hedging"), will buy or sell hundreds of contracts to your one or two. Obviously, your impact is small so you cannot win if you try to fight those large commercial interests. Instead, you should try to go with them.

Determine the trend and go with the trend. Then, like a boat going down river, you sail along with it. Your profits should then increase at a rapid rate.

To fight against that trend is like trying to row that boat upstream. Eventually, you will be exhausted and have to quit.

It is important, therefore, to know whether the market will soon be bullish or bearish and go with that trend— up or down. It is foolish to trade contrary to that trend.

Try to recognize the signs of exhaustion that tell you a bullish move has reached its top. This will protect you from staying in the market too long. It will also help you to make plans to change your thoughts from bullish to bearish. Or, at low prices, from bearish to bullish and go with that new trend whenever it changes.

The "moving averages", explained in Chapter 11, will help you be more certain of the trend. And you will earn more money on each trade if you watch those "moving averages" closely.

RULE 7

IF YOU ARE NOT SURE OF A TRADE
STAY OUT OF THE MARKET

To win, in commodities, the market must move in your favor. When you are not confident you are right, you may look for "news" or "opinions" to give you the confidence you need. You may even ask someone who is no better informed than you are. Sometimes, you may rely upon a broker who is usually too busy answering phone calls and writing up orders during each day to take the time to carefully read the news, study the market, keep up on his charts and analyze the fundamentals.

Ask for opinions, yes. But follow them only if you know the one who gives you his opinion has based that opinion on calm and careful judgment rather than on a quick and uncertain analysis.

RULE 8

DON'T BUY OR SELL UNLESS YOU BELIEVE
YOU CAN EARN A PROFIT OF 60% OR MORE

Never try to "scalp the market". Before you buy or sell, try to make certain the market will move far enough in your favor —up or down—to give you a net profit of 60% or more. This is another good reason why you should always look for and trade in "special situations".

If you follow this rule, you will never be one of those eventual losers who try to take small profits or "scalp the market".

You need to feel there is a possibility you can earn at least 60% or more (after commissions) on each trade you make because, from time to time, you will take some losses. The 60% or more you gain on a good move will help you regain the capital you may lose on a less fortunate trade.

With this rule firmly in mind, you should then be able to earn at least 30% or more per month—360% per year.

RULE 9

NEVER COMMIT YOUR ENTIRE CAPITAL TO ANY ONE TRADE

Always have some capital in reserve. A good rule for a beginner is to use only 75% of the money you have placed on deposit with your broker. If you open your account with $2,000—use only $1,500 to trade. If you have $5,000 in your account—use only $3,750. If you have $10,000—use only $7,500. The other 25% should be kept in reserve until you become more professional and know, for certain, the trend is going to move in your favor.

There are three reasons for this rule.

1. It helps you to trade with less strain. Your mind is able to think more clearly because you are not under pressure to put up more margin for your next trade if you should have a loss on your first trade.

2. If one of your trades should show a loss because you must get out that day, you will then have enough money to make a more favorable trade the next day— or at a later date.

3. You must always have enough money available to take advantage of a "special situation" when it comes along. If all of your capital is tied up in a commodity that moves very little in price, you do not have the extra amount of money you need to take advantage of that opportunity. Instead, you will have to wait until your capital is increased by a price move in your favor—and that may take several days or weeks.

RULE 10

LEARN HOW TO SELL SHORT

To make the maximum amount of money from commodity trading, you must be ready and willing several times each year to sell "short". In fact, you can earn more money— faster—selling short than you can by going long. The reasons are—

1. The general public is usually wrong. They prefer to buy

and hope for higher prices. As prices decline, they get out sometimes with losses. Their sales, plus the sales by professionals who sell short and the "hedge sales" placed by commercial interests speed up the decline.

2. Profits come faster in a declining market. The reason is —prices have to be pushed up, but they fall fast because all that is necessary is for potential buyers to step aside, refuse to buy or drop their bids.

3. Hedging by commercial interests helps the professional "short sellers" add pressure to the market. Until there is less pressure from selling, the market cannot move up.

RULE 11

DON'T GET CAUGHT IN TRAPS

Traps can cause you to lose a large amount of money in a hurry. A "bull trap" occurs when prices break out above an area where price congestion extended over a period of many weeks. Then, one or two days later, The market turns around. Prices go down and sell below the bottom of that congestion. (See Chart A below). When the new low is made, prices generally go down very fast.

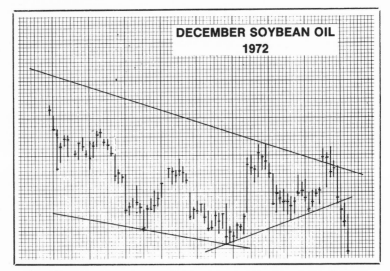

DECEMBER SOYBEAN OIL 1972

A "bear trap" is just the opposite. After prices break below a long area of congestion, they will turn around and go above that trading range. Then they will move higher very rapidly. (See Chart B on next page.)

The losses in each of the above "traps" are so large they usually wipe out most of the capital in a trader's account. That is why you must always guard yourself against getting caught in either a bull or a bear trap.

The most logical way to protect yourself against a "trap" is to go back and read RULE 3 very carefully. If you know what the fundamentals might be in a few weeks or months, you will find it easier to follow the market in the right direction—up or down—and not be caught in a trap.

RULE 12

CUT YOUR LOSSES AND
LET YOUR PROFITS GROW

This is the most important rule of all. It is also the hardest to learn. But you MUST learn this rule—or you will never *build a fortune in commodities.*

Few people have the character, mental stability or the courage to take small losses. If you are one of the few who can do this, you will then stand an excellent chance of earning 360% or more every year.

When most traders make a trade, they believe they are right in their judgment. If the market moves against them, they stubbornly hold on. *They hate to admit they are wrong.* Even when their loss grows larger, they refuse to take that loss and get out. They hope the market will soon turn around and prove they are correct—or—at least move back again so

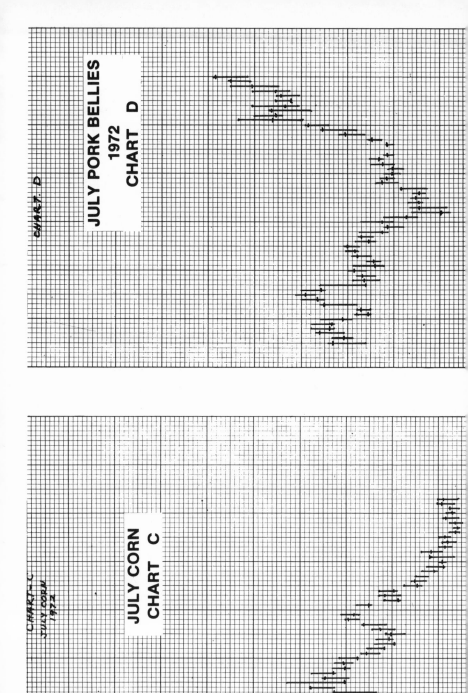

JULY PORK BELLIES
1972
CHART D

JULY CORN
CHART C

their loss will not be as large. But, too often, the market does not return to that level. What happens then?

Obviously, if you are wrong and the market moves against you, your loss may continue to grow until all of the capital in your account is gone.

When you place your order to buy or sell "short", you will usually know whether you are right or wrong before the day is over. If you are wrong and the trade you made shows a loss of 20% or more, you should get out before the close of the market that day. Taking such a loss (before prices move further against you) takes a lot of courage.

To minimize losses, you must analyze the market more carefully. Study the fundamentals. Read RULE 3 once again. You may find that, if you were bullish, you may have to become bearish. If you were bearish, you may need to become bullish. If you reverse your position, the loss you take can soon be made up and a large profit can result from your prompt and courageous decision. The "moving averages," explained on page 145, will help you make this decision more easily and with greater confidence.

For example, Chart C concerns Corn. It shows what happened to thousands of traders who were long and believed prices might move higher to $2.00 per bushel. It only took them a few weeks to lose all of their capital. If, instead, they had ignored the "news" about a possible "corn blight" and sold May Corn "short" 'around 164, they could have had tremendous profits during those same few weeks.

Chart D concerns Pork Bellies. At a price around 28¢ in August, 1971, the news was continually bearish. Very few traders believed that May Bellies would get above 32¢ for a long time. Too many hogs, they said. But prices did rise above 32¢ to 53¢. Those who believed the fundamentals would look better as each month rolled along earned tremendous profits—400% or more). Those who did not believe were "short". They took large losses as their short positions were wiped out.

Chart E concerns Live Cattle. Around the 33.50 level in Early April, 1972, the news given out said, "Consumers are mad about the high prices of beef. Investigations started in Washington. Super-markets running sales at lower prices to satisfy the demand for lower prices." Those who sold short believing the news found they were wrong when the prices of Live Cattle futures continued to go up. And those who knew what the fundamentals might be, a few months later, made large profits of 300% to 500% as they held on and kept buying Live Cattle futures.

When you find you have a profit and prices start to move in your favor, stay with your position. The market may go a long way up—if you get in near the bottom—or—a long way down, if you sold "short" near the top. In either case, stay long or "short" until the market turns around and tells you to get out.

The "moving averages" described in Chapter 11 will help you a great deal to buy near the bottom and sell near the top. You should, therefore, be able to earn a larger amount of profit—more easily.

CHART E

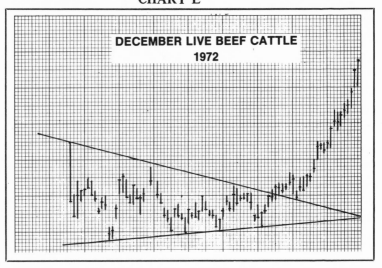

DECEMBER LIVE BEEF CATTLE
1972

When you take large profits in that way, you will overcome many of the small losses you have to take from time to time. In fact—this is the answer to *how to build a fortune in commodities.*

RULE 13
DON'T OVERTRADE

One of the biggest mistakes that amateurs will often make is—they "overtrade".

You overtrade when you trade on too little capital. You overtrade when you have all of your capital tied up in any one trade. You overtrade when you keep jumping "in and out" of the market like a rabbit—hoping for small profits.

You overtrade when you are not sure which way the market might go so—you "guess" and "hope". The result is—you overtrade and, eventually, you lose.

RULE 14

NEVER ANSWER A MARGIN CALL

When a broker calls you for more margin, tell him to close out your position. *You have, obviously, made a mistake.* And you may have violated some of the rules in this chapter—especially Rules 12, 13 and 16. The margin call means you have a large loss. During the next trading day, there is a possibility that your loss may be larger. Take the loss you have and wait a few more days. A better opportunity will come along because a "special situation" is always developing.

If you do not obey this rule, the market will spank you hard in an effort to teach you this fact—*you must always follow the rules or, eventually, you will lose.*

RULE 15

THE MARKET IS ALWAYS RIGHT

All professional traders agree that "the market is always right". The current price is all that matters. If the market goes down when you think it should go up—or—it goes up when you think it should go down—don't argue with the market. Go with it. If you do not like the way the market is acting—get out before your loss becomes greater.

A few days later, you may realize that the fundamentals have changed. And — whenever the fundamentals change — you must change. Your previous analysis must be revised due to the new conditions that affect the market.

RULE 16

WHENEVER A MARKET DOES NOT ACT
AS IT SHOULD — GET OUT

Whenever a market does not act as it should, based on your understanding of the fundamentals and the charts, get out of that market—before it moves to a point where your "stop loss" is caught.

It is wiser to be out of such a market than to be wrong and suffer a loss. Furthermore, when you are out of a market that is "not acting right", you are able to appraise it more clearly. Your judgment can then be based on reason rather than "wishes" or "hope".

This rule helps you save time because, if you bought Soybeans at 3.40 per bushel, Pork Bellies at 36.00 per pound or Cocoa at 30.00 and the price goes down to 3.30; or 35.00; or 28.00, you may have to wait a few days for the market to go back up to the level you bought them. And, of course, it is also possible that the market may never go back to that level during the life of the contract.

But, if the market does go back, the round trip—down then up—is an unnecessary waste of time. You can save that loss of time if you close out your position the first day the market closed at a loss of 20% or more from the price you paid for the contract.

There is another advantage in closing out a trade before it moves further against you. At the lower price (in a declining market), you will have an opportunity to buy at a lower price. Or you can sell at a higher price in a rising market. The extra advantage in price that you gain in this way can help you recover your small loss and, if you are right, it can add that much more profit to your trade.

When you take a small loss, it does not prove you are wrong on which way the market will eventually go. It only means that your judgment concerning when to buy or sell was not perfect. You should wait, therefore, at least two or three more days before you plan to re-enter the market. After two additional days of trading, the market should then be at a point where (1) the price has moved further in that same direction—up or down. Then, when that market turns around, you can earn a larger profit than you could have earned from your first position. Or (2) after another two or three days of trading around that price level, the market may then be more certain to move in the direction you first thought it would move.

RULE 17

DON'T TRY TO AVERAGE A LOSS

As you learned in RULE 16 above, many traders do not have the courage nor the wisdom to admit they are wrong. If a trade goes against them, they will try to "average their loss".

If they are "short" and the market goes higher, they will sell some more. They "hope" for a decline. But that decline may not come. If they sell against the trend and the market goes up instead of down, they will lose on both contracts.

It would be wiser to close out the loss, stay out of the market for a few days and try to determine the trend—up or down.

The "moving averages", explained in Chapter 11 and, especially, the book, *Professional Trading System* (Windsor Books, Box 280, Brightwaters, N.Y., 11718) will help you be more certain of the trend. You can use your capital to better advantage and go with that trend.

RULE 18

DON'T HOLD A POSITION OVERNIGHT IF IT SHOWS A LOSS

If prices near the close of a trading day show that you have a loss of 20% or more—close out your trade. Give your broker an order to "buy or sell at the close" (whichever it might be).

Why? Because, if you buy because you believe the market should move higher—but it does not move higher—you are either wrong in your judgment—or—your timing caused you to buy too soon. Prices may eventually move higher but not as soon as you would like. And you must always realize that —the next day—the market may go "down the limit".

If prices should go lower, the small loss you take by getting out that day can be made up many times over by buying that same commodity at a point somewhat lower the next day or a few days later.

Also, if you sold a commodity "short" because you believed that prices should move lower—but they rise instead of decline—then you were either wrong in your judgment or you sold too soon. Prices may go lower someday, but not as soon as you would like.

If prices should move against you and go higher, the small loss you take by getting out that day can be made up many times over by selling that same commodity at a point somewhat higher a few days later.

Take your small loss and get out. The chances are the market will go a little further in the same direction as the closing trend.

RULE 19

NEVER TRADE ON INCOMPLETE NEWS OR TIPS

Generally, when you find yourself too lazy to analyze the fundamentals, study your charts and make a decision based on careful judgment, you will tend to look for "news" or "hot tips" to give you an idea which way the market might go. When you receive that news or tip, however, the market will usually turn around and go in the opposite direction.

The reason is—the news or the tips you receive will seldom become public information until after a move is near completion. That is why it is so important to study, analyze and try to determine what the fundamentals might be in a few more weeks or months.

"The price of every commodity", as you learned in RULE 3, "will move up or down before the fundamentals are generally known."

RULE 20

DON'T TRY TO BUY AT THE BOTTOM OR SELL AT THE TOP

When Baron Rothschild was asked how he got rich, he replied ,"I never buy at the bottom and I always sell out before prices reach the top." Even Baron Rothschild realized you cannot buy at the bottom nor sell at the top. So forget it. Instead, try to know when the trend is going to reverse and go in the opposite direction. Then go with that trend— up or down — when it comes. The "moving averages", explained in Chapter 11, will help you pin-point that change in trend.

RULE 21

NEVER SELL A NEW HIGH

If the market keeps making new highs, there are good reasons for it. It is wiser to be "long" and go with the uptrend than try to sell "short" and fight against that trend. The fact is—you have no definite way of knowing how high the market may move against you. Wait a few days for a definite indication if a top or a reversal in trend is indicated. It might be several days or weeks away.

A careful study of the 4 day, 9 day and 18 day "moving averages" will help you determine the change of trend more easily.

RULE 22

NEVER BUY A NEW LOW

If the market keeps making new lows, there are good reasons for it. It is wiser to be "short" and go with the downtrend than try to fight against that trend. The fact is—you have no way of knowing how far down the market may go. If you use more of your capital to buy on a declining market and the market continues to decline, the loss you take on both contracts may wipe out your capital.

It is wiser to sell out and take a small loss. Then wait at least two days. If the market looks like it might make a bottom for a move up, buy lightly at that point. But, if the market goes against you on that purchase, remember RULES 12 and 15, close out your position and wait another two days. Eventually, the market may turn and move up.

The primary point is—sell near the close of the trading day if you have a loss of 20% or more after you have bought. But, if the market should go your way and you have a profit, you can then buy more and hold on.

RULE 23

NEVER TRY TO "HEDGE" A LOSS

If you were wrong when you made a trade and prices move against you, don't try to "hedge" or recoup your losses by a trade in the opposite direction. If you do, you ignore RULES 6, 12 and 15.

If you are long and prices go down, don't sell another month "short" and "hope" you will protect yourself against further loss. Or, if you are "short" and the market moves up, don't buy another month and "hope" you will earn a profit on the move towards higher prices. You may earn some money on one side, but you will surely lose on the other.

One loss is difficult enough to accept. Why make it more difficult by trying to be right—twice. It is wiser to be out of the market with a small loss. Then your mind will be free to look for and trade in a "special situation" that may be more certain to move in your favor.

RULE 24

TRADE ONLY WITH SURPLUS FUNDS
DON'T USE MONEY YOU NEED FOR
NECESSARY EXPENSES

If you cannot afford to lose whatever money you have, you will find it difficult to win. The reason is—you will not follow the rules given in this chapter. And, if you fail to follow these rules, you may never have a profit at the end of each year.

RULE 25

TAKE SEVERAL VACATIONS
AWAY FROM THE MARKET EVERY YEAR

This is another important rule that will really pay off in larger profits. In simple words, it means you should know "when to take yourself out of the game".

From a practical standpoint, you should not trade in commodities every day throughout the year. A close and constant study of commodities, day after day and week after week, is mentally very tiring. You will trade more wisely and profit more often if you spend many days and sometimes weeks away from the market. The rest will allow you to come back into the market refreshed.

Good pitchers in ball games have a bad day or get tired. They get the rest they need and try again another day. Lee Trevino, golf's leading money winner in 1971, shot a 75 one day in April, 1972. He quit the tournament he was playing in and said, "I am going home to rest. I'm tired." Then, a few weeks later, he flew to England and won the British Open for the second consecutive year.

In commodities, there may be many times when you will get tired or trade in a careless way because you get so close to the market you cannot see the big moves that are developing. It is wiser, therefore, to take a vacation from trading. A few days later, or even a few weeks later, you will be pleased to find how much clearer your mind has become and how much more easily you can sense which way the trend may move—up or down.

RULE 26

EVERY DAY GIVES YOU A NEW OPPORTUNITY

At the beginning of every day, analyze the market. Determine the amount of capital you have in your account. Make out a definite trading plan. If you made a mistake and lost a day or two earlier, you can make up that loss with a good trade.

If you have a profit, determine whether you should take that profit or enter a "stop loss order" under the low point of the previous day, or a "buy on stop" order above the high of the previous day. Then, let your profits grow as pointed out in RULE 12.

As the market moves along in your favor, your profits should increase each day. Eventually, the market will stop, turn around and move in the opposite direction. At that point, take your profits, reverse your position and go with the new trend.

SUBSCRIBE TO ONE OR MORE ADVISORY SERVICES

If you do not have sufficient know-how or are unwilling to spend the time to learn, hire someone who does have the know-how and the time. Pay him well for his services. It will be one of the best investments you can make.

Subscribe to all the advisory services and chart services you can afford. You can learn much from the better ones. And they are more reliable than the "free" advice you may get because free advice, quite often, has no value. Good advice, on the other hand, is worth all that an advisor asks for it.

Before you subscribe to any service—ask to see a "performance record" of *all their trades* for at least six months to a year.

RULES YOU SHOULD KNOW AND FOLLOW

Read and re-read these rules many times. If you learn them, you may become a professional and win. If you fail to learn these rules, you will remain an amateur and, eventually, you will lose.

1. Have a definite plan and stick to it.
2. Look for "special situations".
3. The price of every commodity moves up or down before the fundamentals are known.
4. Control your emotions.
5. When you make a mistake—admit it.
6. Determine the trend—up or down—then follow it.
7. If you are not sure of a trade—stay out of the market.
8. Don't buy or sell unless you believe you can earn a profit of 60% or more.
9. Never commit your entire capital to any one trade.
10. Learn how to sell "short".
11. Don't get caught in "traps".
12. Cut your losses and let your profits grow.
13. Don't overtrade.
14. Never answer a margin call.
15. The Market is always right.
16. When a market does not act as it should—get out.
17. Don't try to average a loss.
18. Never stay in a position overnight if your loss is over 20%.
19. Never trade on incomplete news or "tips".
20. Don't try to buy at the bottom or sell at the top.
21. Never sell a new high.
22. Never buy a new low.
23. Never try to "hedge" a loss.
24. Trade only with surplus funds. Don't use money you need for necessary expenses.
25. Take several vacations away from the market every year.
26. Every day gives you a new opportunity.
27. Subscribe to one or more advisory services.

EVERY RULE YOU VIOLATE WILL
COST YOU MONEY

11

HOW TO USE CHARTS TO EARN LARGER PROFITS

This book eliminates much of the discussions on charts that have proved to be so time-wasting and costly to the great majority of traders in the past who became confused by following some of the rules and theories in previous books on charts and their analysis.

Too many were "whipsawed". Others fell into bull or bear "traps" when the market moved in the opposite direction from the one the "chart pattern" indicated. In an effort to eliminate that confusion and help you earn a larger amount of profit each year, I have broken this discussion of charts into three parts:

1. This chapter—"How To Use Charts"
2. Chapter 12—"Charts That Indicate When To Buy"
3. Chapter 13—"Charts That Indicate When To Sell"

"Charting" is a technique that requires a combination of work, study, experience, know-how and, possibly, a little ESP (Extra Sensory Perception). The primary purpose of charts is to help you discover a pattern of price movements that indicate which way a market might move—up or down.

No matter how adept you become at "reading a chart", occasionally you will be wrong. In fact, many professional traders who follow charts will readily admit they take losses on 50% of their trades. They say, "If you want to be a successful trader, small losses should always be expected. *It is the large losses you must guard against.*" And that is the basic purpose of these three chapters.

I will, therefore, eliminate a large amount of information, charts and discussions that other books contain. Your goal should be to earn an average of 30% per month—360% per year. To earn that amount, you must look for and trade only in "special situations". For that reason, any ideas, charts or patterns that fail to consider this concept of special situations and earnings of 30% per month, should be forgotten. You will then find it easier to become one of those 10% who make

money in commodities and you will never become one of those
90% who lose.

*   *   *

Timing is important. To be a successful trader, you must
know five things:

1. What to buy.
2. What to sell.
3. When to buy.
4. **When to sell.**
5. When to stay out of the market.

This chapter and the next two will help you make more
money once you gain the knowledge necessary and have a
better feel for which way a market might move—up or down.
Point five above is discussed in Chapter 18, "Tips From A
Professional".

Forecasting the price of commodities is based on two approaches. The technical approach (charts) and the fundamental approach (research analysis, estimates of supply and
demand, government reports, etc.) Experience has shown
that if you want to earn the largest amount of money possible, you should consider both the technical approach and
the fundamentals at the same time.

When you decide to enter the market and take a position,
you are forced to think. You no longer take things for granted.
You try to protect yourself and you seek ways to conserve
your capital. You look for guides and "signals". The easiest
way to do this is through the use of charts.

Charts are helpful because they can improve your timing.
The price movements that are recorded reflect the combined
thoughts and opinions of all the professional traders, speculators and commercial interests involved in the market. (Some
will be right and some of the very best traders will, at times,
be wrong.)

Certain patterns develop that indicate why, at certain price
levels, a commodity should be bought or sold. Professional
traders wait for these patterns to form. And they know that
buying or selling before the time is right or the price is right,
can prove to be costly.

Every professional trader keeps a chart of one kind or
another, or he will subscribe to a "chart service". There are
eight good reasons why:

1. Charts show, at a glance, what the market has done over the past few weeks or year.
2. They give you the exact price level where the market has received the most support.
3. They give you the exact price level where the market has met resistance.
4. They show you whether a commodity, at that time, is active or, temporarily, inactive.
5. They help you know whether a "special situation" is developing.
6. They show you whether the present price information is, primarily, a situation of liquidation (getting out) or accumulation (getting in).
7. They help you determine the best time to buy or sell.
8. They can also help you decide to stay out of the market until a more definite "special situation" develops in that commodity—perhaps in a few more days or weeks.

There is no special magic in charts. Every formation you see has a psychological reason for forming the pattern it makes. When you look at those patterns you can sense a certain amount of strength or weakness in that commodity. This will give you confidence to buy according to that strength or sell according to the weakness you see.

There are only three problems to consider:

1. Which commodity to buy or sell.
2. **What day to buy or sell.**
3. At what price to buy or sell.

The fundamentals and news should always be considered because they help you improve your timing. As a general rule, the market will always reach out to a price level that will justify what the actual fundamentals will be—in the future. (See page 38.) In other words, prices will move in an uptrend to justify a shortage of supply that will occur within a few weeks or months and prices will continue to move downward to justify a larger surplus or a decrease in demand that may occur in a few weeks or months.

If you do not fully understand the importance of the fundamentals and how those fundamentals cause the market to move up or down, you may find your reading of the charts will, sometimes, cause you losses.

You can, therefore, solve most of this problem with this step-by-step plan:

1. Subscribe to a major chart service that will give you charts with the price movements up-to-date on all of the major commodities. (See Chapter 15—"Advisory Services".)

2. Consider the "moving averages" explained later in this chapter. Wait until those "moving averages" tell you that the trend has changed from down to up—or—from up to down.

3. Go over each chart and draw in your trend lines and the most obvious price patterns as pointed out later in this chapter.

4. Pick out "special situations" in 5 or 6 commodities that seem to offer better than average opportunities for large profits.

5. Lay those 5 or 6 charts out on a large table and look at them carefully. On a comparison basis, choose three that look like they might be the best.

6. Remove the other charts. Lay them aside for review later in a few more weeks. Compare each of the remaining three very carefully once again. Pick out no more than two.

7. Now get all the news, information and reports you can find concerning those two commodities. Read them carefully. Analyze the statistics. Try to determine what the supply and demand situation might be in a few more weeks or months. See if the news and statistics give you a feeling about which way the market might move—up or down.

8. Subscribe to the "Commodity Trend Service". When their charts and information arrive, compare it with your own judgment and feelings. This will give you a "third party" viewpoint that should prove to be helpful.

9. Make a decision to trade.

Points 2 and 3 concern the technical aspects of the market. This helps you to know when to buy or sell. And you need to do this on a carefully planned, conservative, basis.

1. On the charts of the two commodities you have selected, draw in the major uptrend or downtrend lines. Then draw in lines to indicate the' most obvious price patterns. These are explained later in this chapter.

2. Next, determine whether the volume and open-interest has been increasing or decreasing over the past few weeks. The wisdom of this and the understanding of its importance was given in Chapter 8.

3. Look for a spot where prices might "break out" in the direction you plan to trade. UP if you want to buy. DOWN if you want to sell.

4. Determine the *minimum profit* (after commissions) — 60%. And your *maximum loss* which should be no more than 20%. Keep those two points firmly in mind because you must always keep your losses small and let your profits grow.

The three most popular types of charts are:
1. The bar chart (daily high-low-close).
2. Point and figure charts.
3. Moving averages based on closing prices.
4. Swing charts. (This type of chart is a modification of the moving average).

THE DAILY BAR CHART

This is the most popular, easiest to use and, in the majority of cases, it is one of the most reliable. The prices you need to fill in the bars each day can be secured from your broker or from the financial pages of your daily newspaper.

POINT AND FIGURE CHARTS

This type of chart is used by many traders, but the following points should be carefully considered:

1. Point and figure charts work best in slow-moving commodities or in stocks. They seldom help you in commodities that tend to move rapidly. Your losses, therefore, might be larger than the 20% maximum you should take.

2. At times, you may find the point and figure chart confusing. It may be difficult to interpret the best time and place to buy or sell.

3. To keep an accurate "point and figure" chart you need to mark down the price of each trade made during each day and determine, accurately, the extent of each price move—up or down. *This is very time-consuming.* A point and figure chart service can do this for you and furnish you with these prices—but they usually arrive several days later. A subscription to this service can be costly and the price changes may

arrive too late for you to complete your charts and determine the best points to buy or sell.

4. In a fast-moving market, it is more difficult to place "stop losses" at the proper points. Prices will oftentimes move above or below those stop points before you can make a decision and inform your broker.

5. Point and figure charts, therefore, should never be used in any commodity that moves fast or has a tendency to have sudden and sharp reversals in price. You will never be able to decide, fast enough, where your order to buy or sell should be. Your losses therefore, will, oftentimes, be larger than the 20% maximum you should take.

In 1962, a test was made of point and figure technique. The results were printed in Fortune Magazine (March, 1962). This test indicated that trades based on point and figure formations returned a profit of 10% - 85% of the time. And losses would have been touched off in 50% of the trades with an average loss of 9.8% after commissions. Obviously, such a poor performance record can not help you earn the potential profit of 30% per month—360% per year that is possible if you select and trade in "special situations."

THE IMPORTANCE OF MOVING AVERAGES

The "moving averages" will help you earn larger profits in both bull markets and bear markets. They take into consideration the two most important elements necessary for profitable trading—time and price change.

Traders who like to earn large profits use the "moving averages" for six reasons:

1. By looking at the moving averages each day, together with their bar charts, they are able to gauge, more accurately, when the trend of the market will turn, definitely, from up to down or from down to up.

2. These moving averages eliminate the wrong opinions, rumors and news that create so much confusion and cause so many losses for the majority of traders who rely, too often, on those wrong opinions, rumors and news.

3. During "trading markets," the price movement patterns you see on a bar chart, can, oftentimes, be deceptive and costly. But traders who use the "moving averages" are able to be more patient.

They also find it is easier to buy or sell with greater confidence.

4. A careful compilation and a constant use of the "moving averages" will point out very clearly why the trend is definitely going to change.

5. The "moving averages" will also help you to know what day the market will break out, decisively, from that confusing and time-wasting trading range.

6. Once the moving averages have pointed out that change in trend, the market will then move strongly and definitely in the direction of that change—either up or down.

The three most popular averages in general use are—the 5 day, the 10 day and the 20 day. I have studied those averages for many years. After much analyzing and checking, I believe your timing of the market can be improved if your averages are based on—4 days, 9 days and 18 days. And, in fast-moving markets (which are the best ones to trade), the extra advantages you gain from that improved timing can give you a considerable increase in profit over the period of one year.

I suggest therefore that you keep a record of the 4 day, 9 day and 18 day averages. If you trade in more than one contract or deal in more than one commodity, the extra profits you gain will make your time and effort worthwhile.

HOW TO COMPILE THE MOVING AVERAGES

To compile the moving averages, you need to buy a dozen or more sheets of 5 x 10 chart paper (size 17 x 22) from any good office supply or art store. You will need one sheet for every commodity you plan to trade. (Any chart paper smaller than 17 x 22 will not give you enough accuracy—and accuracy is always important if you want large profits).

For a starting date, select a Monday and mark that date at the bottom of your chart paper. Then count forward five more squares and mark it for the next Monday. Continue counting five squares and enter the Monday dates for several months in advance. The price range should be marked at the left hand side of your paper in the same way you mark the prices on your bar charts.

To compile the 9 day moving average, select one monthly contract of the commodity you prefer to trade. Add the closing prices for the 9 days previous to that first Monday. Then divide the total of those 9 closes by 9 to get the first point for your 9 day moving average. On the tenth day, add the closing price for that tenth day to the total for the previous 9 days. This will give you a new total. Then subtract the first closing figure of the previous 9 days. Divide this new total by 9 and enter it above the Tuesday line on your chart paper. On the eleventh day, repeat the procedure used for the tenth day. Continue this same procedure every day until that contract goes off the board.

I personally plot only 3 figures on my "moving averages" charts. One figure is the closing price for that day. I mark this down in black ink and keep drawing a line from one black entry to the next day's entry spot. I draw the 9 day average in green ink and the 18 day average in red ink.

The 4 day average is completed in the same way as the 9 day and the 18 day averages. It is not placed on the charts, because you need to consider the 4 day average only near the beginning or end of a move.

For actual samples of the 4 day, 9 day and 18 day "moving averages," write for free sample copy to:

Commodity Trend Service, Inc.
1224 U.S. Hwy., 1-Cove Plaza
North Palm Beach, Fla. 33408

You will receive large, easy to understand charts of the "moving averages" on 20 of the most active commodities. Then you will have a better understanding of how those "moving averages" foretold the change of trend in the past. You will also have a clearer picture of which way the market might move for each one of those 20 markets in the future. This will, obviously, improve your timing and increase your profits.

When you compile your moving averages, you will find that, whenever the trend changes from down to up, the closing prices and the 4 day average will move sharply ahead of the 9 day average. The 18 day average will lag far behind. This will continue until the closing price and the 4 day average move closer together. The 9 day average will then gain rapidly and the 18 day average will also pick up speed.

It may take several weeks for a top or a bottom to be completed. During that time, a "trading market" will usually occur in which the closing prices, the 4 day and the 9 day average seem to move up, down and around one another. The 18 day average, however, will continue to gain until, finally, th 18 day will pull up even with the 4 day and the 9 day. At that point, you may be certain the market has lost its momentum. The trend will then begin to change—usually within one or two days.

To double check this change in trend and make certain it will move in your favor, study your bar charts. Also turn to Chapter 8 and consider the meaning of the changes in volume and open-interest over the previous weeks or months.

HOW TO USE THE MOVING AVERAGES

Whenever the 4 day average moves above the 9 day average, a "watch to buy" signal is given. When the 4 day average moves below the 9 day average, a "watch to sell" signal is given. These "signals" mean that the "trading market" during the past 9 trading days may be coming to an end.

To make a successful trade, however, you need to wait for a more definite, clear-cut signal that such a "trading market" has come to a final end. The market should then move, more decisively, in one direction.

A clearcut "buy signal" comes on the day when the 4 day average moves above the 9 day average and the 9 day average moves above the 18 day average.

When the market moves steadily upward, the 18 day moving average will trail behind. As the top approaches, the 9 day average will begin to slow down. It will then, slowly, make a rounding top and seem to stop moving higher. When that occurs, the 18 day average gains ground on the 9 day average, moves closer to it and, eventually, moves above that 9 day average.

The first day the 9 day average moves below the 18 day average you then have a signal to take profits on all of your long positions and "sell short".

Note: As a final double check, make certain the 4 day moving average (a simple average which you keep each day but do not place on your chart) is also below the 9 day average or the downtrend could be a false move. If it is, you should wait, temporarily, for another day or two until all of the signals given above confirm the end of the bull move and the beginning of the bear move.

A clear-cut "sell signal" comes when the 4 day average moves below the 9 day average and the 9 day average moves below the 18 day average.

In a bear market, the 9 day average will move steadily down and the 18 day average will lag behind. As the bear market ends, the 9 day average slows down, makes a rounding bottom and seems to stop moving lower.

The first day the 9 day average moves above the 18 day average, you then have a signal to take profits on all of your "short positions" and buy for the next bull move.

Note: As a double check, make certain the 4 day moving average is also above the 9 day average or the new bull move could be a false one. If it should be a false move, wait for another day or two until all of the signals given above confirm the fact the end of the bear market has arrived and a new bull market is about to begin.

It requires a considerable amount of time and effort to compile these 4 day, 9 day and 18 day averages, place them on your charts and analyze them. But, if you want to gauge, more accurately, the time to buy or sell with the maximum potential for profit, you will find the extra time and effort you give to this work is worthwhile.

To save time in the future and give yourself a double check on the trend of the market, you should keep the 4 day, 9 day and the 18 day moving averages on at least two different months for at least 14 of the most active commodities. The two charts should be at least six months apart. December and July for example. November and May. In Pork Bellies and Live Hogs, use February and August. In Live Cattle use April and October.

Furthermore, if you want to find and trade in the best "special situations", the 4, 9 and 18 day moving averages should be kept on at least 14 of the 20 major commodities because, from time to time, you will need to move from an indecisive "trading market" into one of the faster-moving "special situations". And, of course, one of the ways you can get a more accurate "feel" of each market is to look at your charts on all of those 14 moving averages. It will help you to spot those special situations more easily.

If you do not have the time to put down the closing figures every day, compile the three averages and make up your charts, you can subscribe to the "Commodity Trend Service". (See Chapter 15.) They will do this work for you at an unusually low cost.

After you find that the trend of the market has definitely changed to a bull move, for example, stay long. Continue to buy on every reaction. Do not consider selling until the 4 day average closes below the 9 day and the 9 day average moves definitely below the 18 day average. And, of course, the reverse is true in a bear market.

This common sense way of trading eliminates most of the confusion that often exists. It offers a more conservative way to trade. It also helps you to know when the top of a market has been made and the next bear trend is ready to get underway. The "moving averages", therefore, can help you take a larger percentage of profit out of the market and help you earn a few thousand dollars in extra profit every year.

As pointed out earlier in this book, no one can "guess" the final top or bottom of the market, but years of experience has proved that the largest and safest profits always come from taking a large profit out of the middle—between the tops and the bottoms. The 4, 9 and 18 day moving averages help you do this.

COMPUTERS

The problem with computers and computer trading is—the computer is set up and programmed by human beings. The value of a computer, therefore, depends on the ability of the individual who sets up the programs and supplies the computer with information. This means that, in commodity trading the programmer has to be an individual with a keen knowledge of the fundamentals for every commodity and have an understanding of why, at certain times, the fundamentals will often change in spite of the way the computer is programmed.

If the information put into the computer is not carefully reasoned out, the results may not be satisfactory. There are several commodity advisory services that use a computer to give their advice but, to date, I have not found one that can offer a record of large profits, often enough, to offset the losses to' assure a net gain of at least three to one.

PROTECT YOURSELF WITH STOP LOSS ORDERS

When most traders take a position, they "hope" the market will move in their favor. But, if prices move against them, they will, too often, hold onto a losing position. Their losses grow larger and their capital grows smaller.

There is no foolproof system for trading just as there is no perfect solution in the professions of medicine, philosophy or law. Mistakes will be made in spite of your knowledge and training. To protect yourself against any error in judgment (and all professionals make an error in judgment from time to time), you need a "stop loss order" on every trade you make.

You can never tell what may happen. That is why "stop loss orders" take care of many "ifs" and "whens" that sometime occur overnight. Unexpected news can, oftentimes, upset both the fundamentals and the charts.

A "stop loss order" is an order to buy or sell "at the market" when the market reaches a specified price. A "buy on stop" order is placed above the market before prices move sharply higher. A "sell on stop" order is placed at a price below the market before prices move sharply lower.

If the market continues to move down, your stop will never be touched for several days or weeks. But, if the market should decline in the morning, then turn around and close higher that day, it will generally mean the decline is over for awhile. And the "stop loss order" you had placed at a price just over the high of the previous day will take you out of the market with a reasonable amount of profit.

Then, after you are closed out with this profit—*take a rest*. Stay out of that market for at least a few days until you can find another "special situation"

WHERE TO PLACE A STOP LOSS ORDER

Many traders place their "stop loss" orders in the wrong place. That is why they are stopped out, so often, with no profit or a loss. After the weak traders are stopped out, the market will usually turn around and go the other way. The traders who are stopped out now see they were right in their judgment and they wish they had placed their stops at a different price. To correct this, remember these four points:

1. A stop loss order should be placed below a support level or above a resistance point.

2. Make certain your stop is somewhat below the up-trend line in a bull market and just above the down-trend line in a bear market.

3. As the market moves up and away from the support level in a bull market cancel your original stop loss order and enter a new stop loss order a few points higher—*every day*. (A minimum of 10 points in commodities that trade in points and ¼¢ in grains.) If you are short, you must lower your stop loss by those same amounts—*every day*.

4. When you are "stopped out", stand aside. Do not trade in that commodity for a few days. This will give you time to look for another and, possibly better, "special situation."

Commodity markets seldom respond smoothly and consistently to the actual fundamentals of supply and demand. Unforeseen events, unexpected news, strikes and political decisions can change the course of any commodity market sometimes overnight. At such times, it is necessary to always be aware of a possible reversal in prices.

What goes up (according to the fundamentals) goes down and what should go down—goes up. That is why an understanding of charts and the "moving averages" can help you decide when to buy or sell regardless of what the fundamentals might indicate.

That does not mean the fundamentals are not important. They are. But, primarily, on a long-term basis rather than on a day to day basis. Generally speaking, commodity markets always turn up or decline ahead of the fundamentals. The reason is—the important commercial interests who are always large buyers or sellers make plans to buy or sell according to what their needs may be—in the future. If they expect prices in a few more months to be higher, they may place "buying hedges" to protect themselves against that possible increase. If they expect prices to be lower in a few more months, they may place "selling hedges" to protect themselves against that possible decline.

If your charts indicate a move towards lower prices and the fundamentals in a few weeks indicate the supply will increase and the demand will be less, then you should sell that commodity "short" and take advantage of the coming decline.

If you trade without considering the "moving averages", don't expect your timing to be perfect. And don't expect an immediate decline after you sell short. If your sale was premature, you may have to wait a few days or weeks for the top to be completed. A careful study of the "moving averages," however, will eliminate this problem to a large extent and your timing will, therefore, be improved.

ONLY THREE TRENDS TO CONSIDER

There are only three basic trends to consider in a commodity market. The uptrend, the downtrend and the horizontal (which many people call "a trading market").

1.   The uptrend. In this trend, prices rise due to the fact there are more buyers than sellers. Demand, therefore, is greater than the supply. You should buy as close to the beginning of this trend as possible and hold your position until the market indicates a top is being made.

2. The downtrend. In this trend, prices decline because the supply is greater than the demand. There are more sellers, therefore, than buyers.

3.   The horizontal trading market. An uptrend or a downtrend will, oftentimes, be interrupted and the direction will be somewhat horizontal. When this occurs, a "trading market" begins. Prices will then rise and fall in an indecisive manner. One reason for this is the supply is, temporarily, equal to the demand and there is no great rush to buy or to sell.

When a trading market occurs, you will receive a buy signal one day then, a few days later, you will receive a sell signal. If you try to change direction each time this occurs, you will be "whipsawed". And, if you are whipsawed too often, you can lose all your capital.

Most commodities spend about 70% of their time each year in those indecisive trading markets. At such times, they should be left alone. They are not worth the time and effort. And, too often, you wind up with losses. They have importance and value only to the commercial interests (farmers, producers, processors, shippers and exporters) who need such a market for good and practical business reasons.

During the remaining 30% of the time, large profits are possible. Eventually, a "special situation" is created. Prices will break out of the trading range—either up or down—you will then have an opportunity to earn a tremendous amount of money in only a few weeks. The charts in Chapters 12 and 13 illustrate many of these "special situations". And the "moving averages" will usually give you a reliable "signal" one or two days before that breakout will occur.

TREND LINES

Markets turn slowly from bullish to bearish and from bearish to bullish. Like a car going down the road, the market slows down, makes a turn in a sort of wide circle, goes back in the same direction from which it came and picks up speed once again in the opposite direction. (The charts in Chapters 4 through 7 help to illustrate this.)

When prices move in a particular direction for a considerable time, it is called a "trend". And, once the direction of the market is established, commodity prices have a strong tendency to continue in that direction.

In a bull move, prices move up in a jagged, zig-zag manner. Each decline makes a bottom higher than the previous bottom. After prices have made a new high, a reaction sets in. Then prices move up again to a point above the previous high. Trend lines can then be established. To be valid, they should connect at least three higher bottoms in a bull market and three lower tops in a bear market.

A line can be drawn from the first bottom to the bottom of the reaction. This is called a "trend line". If the reaction stops at, or close to that line, the trend line is considered valid. Every decline from that point on should stop at that uptrend line.

Occasionally, a nearly perfect bull move will occur. In this type of move, all the highs and lows seem to fit into a pattern which is called a "channel". (See Chart below.) In these situations, you buy (in a bull market) every time the market declines to a price near the bottom of that channel. And, in a bear market, you sell every time the market rallies to a point near the top of the channel.

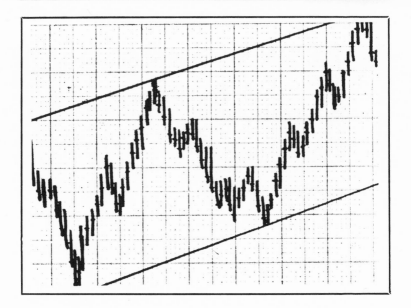

Even when the trend is definitely up, the market will not continue to trade in that direction without an occasional pause. There will be times when prices will reverse. These reverses (declines in a bull market) are caused by a condition where there are, temporarily, more orders to sell than there are orders to buy. And, in a declining market, the market will often move up (rally) two or three days because there are, temporarily, more orders to buy around that level than there are orders to sell.

Such reverses in trend cause a zig-zag pattern. The reason is—during each day, many traders and commercial interests are willing to sell and their sales slow down the market (in a bull market) and prevent it from going straight up. The sales come from commercial interests who need to place "short hedges" to carry on their business, scalpers (floor traders) who hope to profit from a small decline and traders who are willing to take a profit on a purchase they made several days or weeks ago.

Look for a major trend to develop. Then go with that trend. Such major trends will develop a more positive force and they are not as likely to turn around and move against you. Instead, they will continue to move in the direction they have started until they complete their major objective.

The profits that result may be as high at 200% to 300% in only a few months.

The two most important trend lines are (1) the Bullish Support Line and (2) the Bearish Resistance Line. (See charts on next page.) From those basic lines, other lines will appear. These new trend lines make a "fan". They indicate that prices will soon move faster in that direction.

As you can see, you can make a large amount of money if you follow that trend for several weeks or months. But to make certain you **are** in the right trend, you need to give each commodity enough time for a trend to develop. This means you should never try to make money trading the minor trends that occur, so often, in trading markets.

Trend lines that are begun at points near a historic low or **historic high are the most reliable spots to lay your plans to buy or sell. The reason is—prices will seldom go below those historic lows (except when there is an unusually large supply of that commodity). And they will seldom go above those highs (except when there is an unusual shortage and a great demand for a commodity). Other elements that can cause markets to go above or below previous historic highs and lows are—wars, severe weather conditions or serious market problems in several foreign countries.**

As long as prices remain above the trend lines indicated in the bullish charts in Chapter 12, stay long. And, you should stay short while prices continue to remain below the trend lines indicated in the bearish charts in Chapter 13. Once these lines are penetrated on the downside of the bullish trend line, sell out your long positions. Then make plans to go short—if the "moving averages" indicate a definite change **in trend. News will soon be coming to explain why the trend** in the market should change. And, once prices move over the bearish resistance line in a bear market, buy back your shorts and go long.

When you study several hundred charts of different commodities, you soon realize that when a trend is either up or down, that trend will continue to move in the same direction until the "moving averages" indicate a definite change in trend.

Uptrend lines with markets moving to progressively higher levels are shown on charts in Chapter 12. Downtrend lines with markets moving to progressively lower levels are shown on charts in Chapter 13.

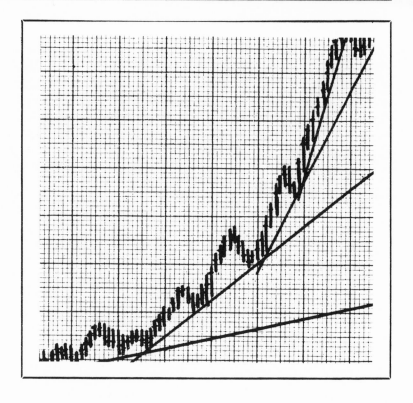

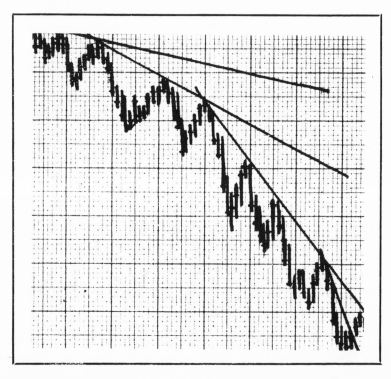

After an uptrend of several months, the bull market comes to an end. A bearish trend begins when, for the last time, prices make a lower bottom after making a lower top. This tells you that the supply of that commodity has overcome the demand. A downward move is indicated. You may then "sell short" provided you protect yourself against any unexpected reversal of trend. You do this by entering a "buy on stop" just a little below the high of the previous move.

THE SIX MOST RELIABLE CHART PATTERNS

Many thousands of traders use charts and the majority of them buy or sell according to certain "signals." You can see, therefore, that once you learn these signals, you will understand why prices will, so often, follow certain patterns and move up and down as they do.

When new fundamental information develops, there is often a divergence of opinion that includes commercial and speculative interests alike. Charts will, oftentimes, tell you which opinion will probably win. But—beware of "traps."

Analysts who use charts believe they can foretell the future direction of the market by studying the patterns which are created when prices are charted each day.

There are six patterns or signals to watch for. Over a period of many years of study, I find these six patterns are, generally the most reliable.

1. The triangle
2. The rising wedge—prepare to sell
3. The declining wedge—prepare to buy
4. The pennant
5. The flag
6. The breakaway gap.

There are other formations discussed in books that you may buy and read if you so desire. But time and experience have proved that most of the money lost by commodity traders has occurred when trading in those formations. For that reason, they are not considered in this book because—in order to *build a fortune in commodities*—you must look for and trade only in "special situations".

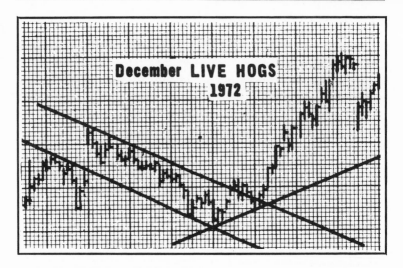

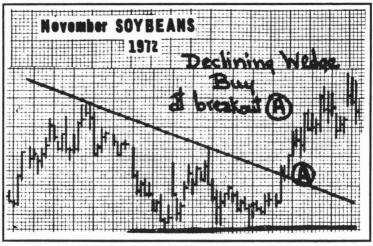

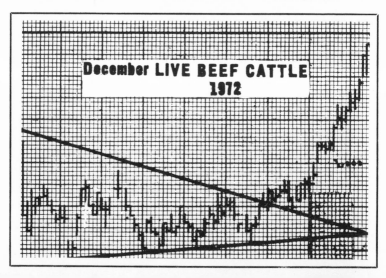

TRIANGLE

Triangles are one of the safest forecasting patterns. They are caused by the difference of opinion between the bulls and the bears. Each of those traders has set opinions and they are reluctant to give much ground. This results in a slow, indecisive but definite narrowing of the trading range. This indecisive "trading market" creates a triangle.

Eventually, something has to happen. After several weeks of trading, some important news or event will cause prices to break out of that triangle.

Triangles always indicate the possibility of a "special situation" so search your charts for them. Two examples are given on the opposite page to show you how triangles may look on your charts. (Other examples are given in Chapters 12 and 13.)

PENNANT OR FLAG

After a market has had a sharp move up or down, a period of consolidation may occur. This will sometimes create a pattern called a pennant or a flag. Watch the volume during the days in these formations. During a true bull market, the volume should be larger on the up days and smaller on the down days. During a bear market, the volume should be larger on the down days and smaller on the up days.

Pennants or flags are not as reliable as "triangles", but they occur often. Prices will usually move out of a pennant or a flag in the same direction as the major trend that preceded it. An UP Pennant and a DOWN Pennant are shown on page 156.

As a general rule, however, the chart formations given in Chapters 12 and 13 will prove to be 70% to 90% accurate. And, if you use them together with the "moving averages", you will find your profits will always be considerably larger than your losses.

CLIMAX FORMATIONS

When a market gains momentum, something is causing it to move faster. After prices break through the top line of a channel in a rising market or break below the bottom line of a channel in a declining market, an "overbought" or "oversold" situation results. Within one or two days, the market will usually move in the opposite direction.

HEAD AND SHOULDERS

In books written previous to this, a head and shoulders formation was always considered reliable. But, occasionally, a head and shoulders formation does not hold up. Notice the chart on December Soybean Oil below. A good head and shoulders bottom was broken in this commodity and another decline set in. The fundamentals were still so "bearish" in Soybean Oil that prices broke down under the right shoulder and destroyed that so-called "strong formation".

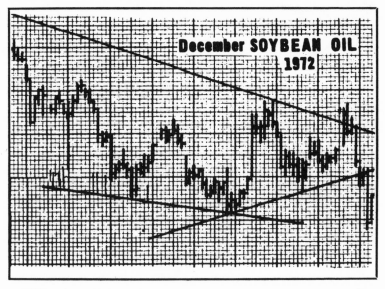

This proved the value of two important points. (1) The fundamentals should always be considered and (2) Close "stop losses" can save you from bigger losses—especially if the fundamentals still rule the market as they did at that particular time.

It is important to note that the weakness in Soybean Oil at that time came in spite of the strong uptrend in both Soybeans and Soybean Meal that moved prices in both those commodities to the highest price levels in their history.

You must clearly understand and realize that no chart formation offers a reliable, unfailing signal. In fact, no chart pattern has ever proved to be 100% right. Occassionally they will be wrong. And, worst of all, they may prove to be wrong at a time when you were certain you were right. That is the reason you must always use "stops" and know where those "stops" should be.

HOW FAR WILL PRICES MOVE

Never try to "guess" how high or low prices may go. Your profits will be larger and more certain if you follow the trend until it changes. This is one of the advantages of the "moving averages", explained on page 145. They help you know, with a greater degree of accuracy, when the trend has definitely changed from down to up or from up to down.

Tops and bottoms can never be accurately determined because price trends follow no definite scientific formula—even though some of the older traders and a few advisory services seem to believe they do. That is why so many of the best professionals admit they take losses—sometimes 50% of the time. (See Chapter 18.)

At times, their "rules" will work. At other times they will not. And, at those times when they do not, you can lose a considerable amount of money. So don't guess. It is wiser to stay out of a certain commodity and not trade than it is to be hard-headed and wrong.

How far each move will continue is difficult to predict. But you can gauge the move, to some extent, by understanding what the fundamentals might be and drawing short-term trend lines to let you know when the decline or rally has exhausted itself.

The safest time to buy or, sell is when the "moving averages" definitely indicate a change in trend. A careful look at the three "moving averages" every day can save you much time and frustration. They eliminate the wild movements, the "whipsaws" and the false moves that often occur when a market is near a top or bottom—just before a change in trend. And, most important, if you understand the fundamentals and realize you are trading in a "futures" market, the "moving averages" will help you stay out of the "traps" that cause so many large losses for traders who rely too much on some of the rules and information given in older books that apply to charts.

It seems that, each year, "traps" occur more often. One reason, perhaps, is too many traders place too much faith in charts and not enough on the fundamentals which must always be considered if you want to be truly successful trading in "a futures market".

As prices climb higher, many traders who have been on the sidelines now enter the market. When the top of the market comes and prices begin to move lower, the small, inexperienced traders get caught. They have never conditioned themselves to "sell short". And, worst of all, most brokers find it difficult to be bearish. Usually, they do not know how to analyze the fundamentals.

Such brokers unwisely advise their customers to "hold on." Soon it is too late. The sell orders begin slowly. They grow larger as prices decline. Then they end up in a panic as prices drop rapidly.

"Guessing" where the final top or bottom might be can prove to be very costly. It will be wise, therefore, to let the "moving averages" help you decide which day and at what time the change in trend—from down to up or from up to down—might be.

This fact concerning the "moving averages" has proved to be reliable one hundred times or more over the past few years —especially in the fast-moving markets where big profits occur for those who are right and large losses occur for those who are wrong.

Only a careful reading of the charts and the "moving averages," together with an appraisal of the fundamentals, the open-interest and volume, can help you gauge which way the market might move and how far that move might carry.

Chapter 13 will give you ideas that can help you know how to sell short and profit from the decline.

The volume of sales in triangles, flags or down pennants will generally grow less each day. Then, when the market breaks out of that formation, the volume of sales should increase at a rapid rate. This indicates a strong market and you should go along with it. Don't consider taking profits or selling "short" until the "moving averages" show that the trend in that market has definitely turned from up to down. This may be several weeks after you have made your purchase.

If a final top has not been made in that market, prices may move indecisively in a trading range for a few weeks. If that trading range should last for several weeks, the time and money you can lose is not worth the frustration nor the effort. You should be out of that market and try to find a "special situation" in another commodity.

PROTECT YOURSELF AGAINST FALSE MOVES.

You must always protect yourself against false moves or "traps." There is no scientific, certain way you can analyze charts and profit from that analysis every time. Occasionally, all markets will move contrary to what the charts indicate.

As the feelings, judgment and beliefs of buyers and sellers change, their orders to buy or sell will create new patterns on the charts. Over a period of several weeks, those patterns will give you a reasonably good indication of which way the next move of the market might be—up or down.

The wise trader will take a longer look at the fundamentals and see why the market did not follow through as his charts indicated. If he does this, he will find that the fundamentals in the market indicated a continuation of the long-term trend.

Many of those chartists who are hard-headed or in love with their charts, will hold on as the market reverses itself and goes against them. Two cases are illustrated on page 156.

Notice in each case that the trend lines were broken. To a "chartist", this means the bull move will turn to a bear and a bear move will turn into a bull move. A few days later, however, the market turned around and continued on its way— in spite of the break in that trend line. This is called "a trap". And those "traps" occur quite often whenever many "chartists" ignore the fundamentals.

To increase your profits and keep your losses as low as possible, take positions in "special situations" selected only after the direction of the move you desire has been confirmed by the "moving averages" (See pages 142-147).

The reason is—in trading markets or other situations, you can never be certain of the direction the market will take. You may, therefore, lose more times than you win. Chapters 12 and 13 will help you know how to select a "special situation" so that, if you are right, you will earn a larger amount of profit.

12

CHARTS THAT INDICATE WHEN TO BUY

Charts, by themselves, can never tell you definitely which way a commodity might move—up or down. So, when a chart pattern develops that indicates a "special situation", study the fundamentals. This is the time when you gain the maximum amount of good from your charts.

If the fundamentals concerning a commodity indicate the demand for that commodity will be greater in a few weeks or months, then prices will move up to justify that fact. Patterns that develop on your charts will indicate that possibility. (See page 38.) If the fundamentals also agree with your chart pattern, buy that commodity. Later, after the market has risen, "the news" will give you the reason why your decision was wise.

After a long bear market of several weeks to several months, watch the "moving averages" for a comparatively safe point to buy. The "moving averages" will give you plenty of warning that a new up-move is coming. And, if you watch those "moving averages" carefully (see information in Chapter 11), you should be able to earn a profit from any "short sales" you may have. Those "moving averages" will also give you a good indication of the best day to buy and go long and benefit from the new move towards higher prices.

The more you understand and know about charts, volume and open-interest, the easier it will be to trade successfully upon what you read. A bull move is indicated when a higher bottom is followed by a higher top. As long as prices make higher bottoms and higher tops, you can conclude that the demand for that commodity has, at that point in time, overcome the supply. The accumulation period by those "in the know" has been completed and prices should continue to move higher.

The price movements that offer big profits take time to complete—usually from 5 weeks to 5 months. Once you have established a good position and you are right with the trend, place a "stop loss" order just below the low point of the last

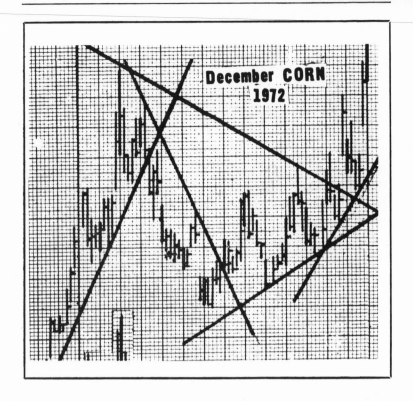

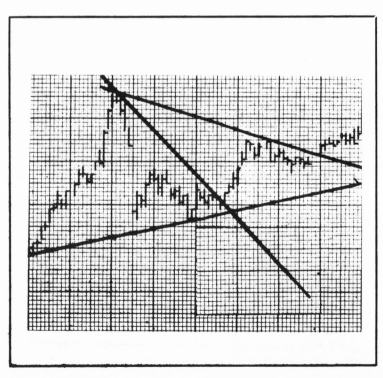

decline. Then walk away from that market. Let it go your way—if it will. If your profits increase, move your "stop loss" higher every week.

When the market starts to move in your favor, study the "moving averages". Each day the market progresses, you will notice how much more confidence you gain by being right with "the trend". Those "moving averages" will, eventually, give you a dependable signal to let you know when you should take your profits.

And those "moving averages" will, eventually, give you a "signal" to sell short and profit from the next decline.

If prices have already made a bottom formation, buy when you find a "triangle," a "flag" or a "down pennant" has developed. The "moving averages" will help you time your purchase so you will be more certain to get in before the bull move actually starts.

One of the best times to buy (and the hardest one to learn) is to buy when prices are at a low point because "the news is bad." After several months of trading at a comparatively low level, prices may create a "declining wedge." As prices move toward the point of that wedge, the volume of sales and the open-interest may decrease. Buy at any time near the point of the wedge and hold—or—buy at any time that prices break out above that long downtrend line. This "special situation" gives you a good opportunity to profit from the advance in prices which must occur sometime soon.

The "declining wedges" in the charts on the previous page illustrate this point.

A break-out on the upside may seldom have a rapid move. The rise in price comes more slowly because prices in a bull market must always be built up. Unlike the speculators, the commercial interests who are short through hedges placed to protect their business (see Chapter 3), are in no hurry to buy back those hedges. As prices rise, the value of the products they have to sell will also rise. The loss they must take on their "short hedges" will, therefore, be small and never as severe as the loss that a speculator will have to take from that same adverse move in price. In fact, the commercial interests who deal in that commodity can wait until the market has risen for several weeks or months before they decide to buy back their "short hedges".

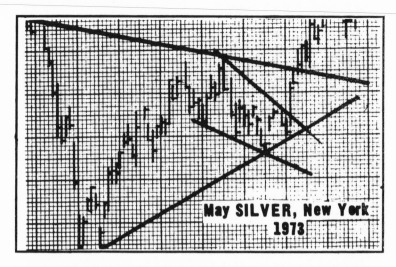

May SILVER, New York
1973

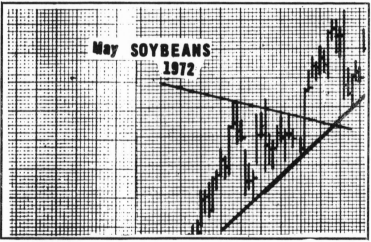

May SOYBEANS
1972

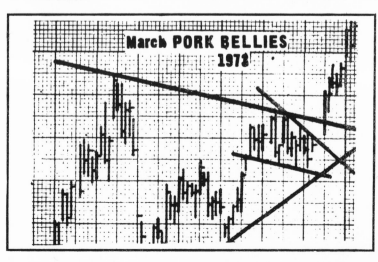

March PORK BELLIES
1973

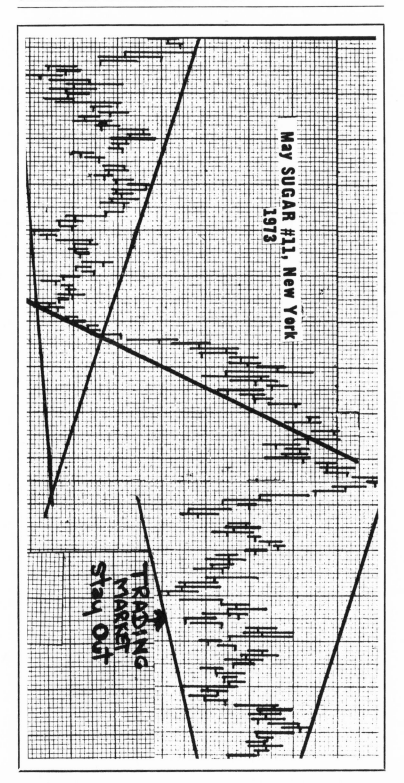

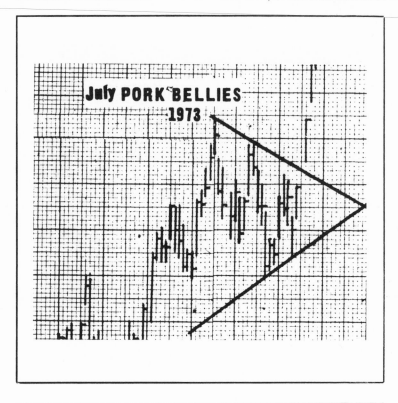

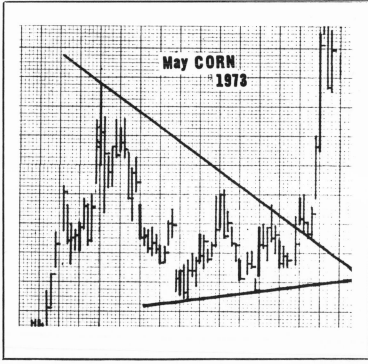

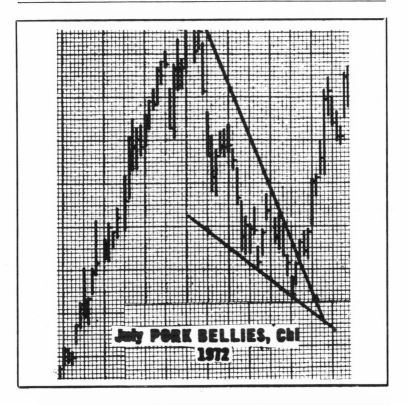

July PORK BELLIES, Chi
1972

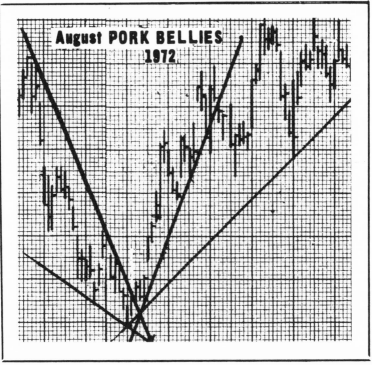

August PORK BELLIES
1972

When a decline comes in a bull market orders come in from more commercial interests that buy back their "selling hedges", other commercial interests enter new "buying hedges", short-term traders buy back their "short sales" and other traders who feel more confident that a bull move is underway will buy in anticipation of higher prices.

As a general rule, each new support area helps to create a sharper angle to the up-trend line. And, as more confidence in the bull move develops, speculators enter the market in larger numbers. Commercial interests add more power to the uptrend as they decide they must buy to fulfill their needs before prices move much higher. All of this increased interest in this market will cause an increase in the total open-interest.

This general enthusiasm and willingness to buy continues to increase until a top has been reached. At that point, a trading market begins. Distribution sets in as the "longs" who are satisfied with their profits sell out to others who waited to buy until they were more certain the news would be good.

13

CHARTS THAT INDICATE WHEN TO SELL

Prices usually fall faster than they rise. Short-sellers therefore, can usually earn more profit in a shorter period of time. A break-out on the downside is usually more reliable than a breakout on the upside. The reason is—most speculators prefer to be long, not short. Most of the large commercial interests, however, will be short—especially near the top of a move. A decline in price, therefore puts pressure on the longs. They may be forced to sell and their sales, together with additional short sales by the commercial interests, will help to speed up the decline.

The small trader finds it difficult to profit from a declining market. And worst of all, he will rarely, if ever, sell a commodity short—even though the fastest profits in all commodity markets will usually come from "short sales"

When a small trader feels that prices are headed lower, he will usually stand aside and wait until he thinks a bottom has been made. At that point, he may take a new long position and try to profit from a potential rise in price. But, if that market should be in a definite bear trend, he may see the market decline once again and be caught with a loss as prices move toward lower levels. That fact is one of the most important reasons why every trader must understand "bear markets" and learn how to "sell short".

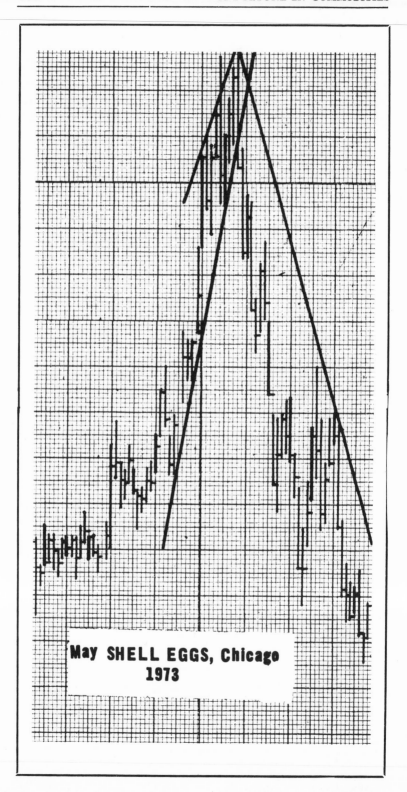

May SHELL EGGS, Chicago
1973

Many "chartists" lose out in such a market and you may too. The safest and most practical way to overcome this problem and make certain you are on the right side of the market is to watch the 4 day, 9 day and 18 day "moving averages" very carefully. Those "moving averages" will always give you a reliable signal—especially if you follow those "averages" as explained in Chapter 11.

In the majority of cases, the market will continue to decline, as it should, from that "rising wedge" and you should stay short and profit from that decline until the "moving averages" point out the day when the decline is definitely over. Then stay out of that market for a few days and look for another "special situation". You will always find one is developing in some other commodity.

To sell "short" successfully, select a commodity that had a large rise over a period of several weeks or months. If the rise was on a large volume and an increase in the open-interest, this means an increased number of speculators. Prices will fall rapidly once the top has been completed because those who are long will sell to protect their losses. Some who bought near the top will sell before their losses are too large. Others will sell as prices continue to decline.

After the commercial interests who were long have been satisfied, professional short sellers will start a selling campaign. Their efforts combined with the sales that come from commercial "hedgers" will put pressure on the market and prices will decline.

If, however, you get a signal that the "moving averages" have definitely made a top and a bear trend will soon be underway, sell that commodity "short." Then hold that short position, until several months later the "moving averages" tell you the market has changed once again from bearish to bullish.

If you are "short", your stop loss order should be just above the top of the resistance level. Then, as the market moves lower and away from that resistance level, cancel your original stop loss order and enter a new stop loss order a few points lower *every day*. Keep lowering your stop loss in this way. When the market begins to move fast on the downside, lower your stop until it is *just a little above the close of the previous day*.

If your "stop loss" is hit, take your profit. Then do not

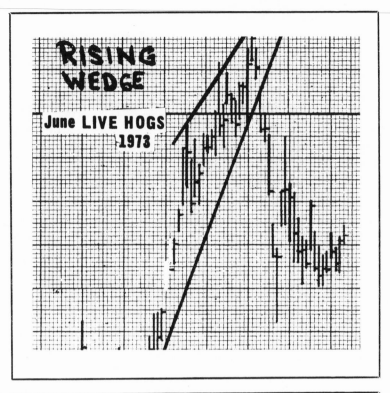

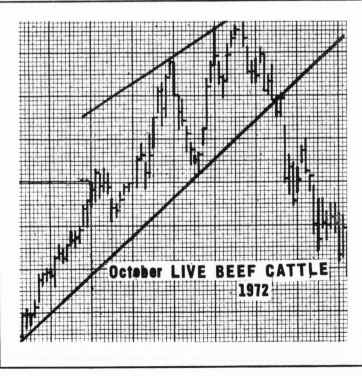

trade in that commodity for at least one or two weeks. A "trading market" may develop. Stand aside, therefore, and wait for a new "special situation" to develop—or—look for a "special situation" in another commodity.

After a commodity has moved continuously higher for a period of several weeks or months, a "rising wedge" may appear. This indicates a good opportunity for a comparatively safe sale. The decline from a rising wedge is, oftentimes, very fast and large profits can be secured in only a few weeks.

While that is true, one big problem exists. You may see this rising wedge forming and decide to sell short. If you sell short a few days or a few weeks before that final top has been completed, prices may continue to be firm or rise (still within that "wedge"). And, occasionally, in very strong markets prices may have one final last move towards new highs. In other words, prices may break out above the top line of the wedge for a few days. If you are not properly margined, your broker may find it necessary to buy back your shorts "at the market". This can add further strength to the upward move and can cause you to lose a great deal of money. After all those "weak shorts" are out of the market and there are no more anxious buyers left to support that market, prices will then fall rapidly from that new high.

The decline you had expected may then begin that same day or the next but, of course, you would be out of that market. You would have less money available to take advantage of that new bear trend and all of the study and effort to find this "special situation" would be wasted. The market will then move along without you.

As a general rule, all sell signals are confirmed when the market dips below the support line. But that confirmation is never definite nor positive every time. When an uptrend line is broken, many "longs" get out. Other traders will "sell short" on that "signal." But there will be times when those signals will prove to be wrong. And, at such times, you must be alert, see the mistake other traders have made, immediately get out of your "short," reverse your position, take your small loss and "go long." Then place a "stop loss" just below the price made by the last low. The charts on the opposite page illustrate how fast prices can fall from a rising wedge.

14

WHY NOT START
A COMMODITY TRADING CLUB?

Everyone wants to earn more money. The problem is—how can it be done if your income is small or your capital is limited?

As this book points out, trading in commodities can be both interesting and profitable—once you know how. Several million men and women, therefore, may decide to trade in commodities. Certain facts, however, must be considered.

1. All commodity brokers are busy during the trading day with many details. Their time, therefore, is limited.
2. The majority of brokers will not accept small accounts under $5,000.
3. They know it is difficult for anyone to earn large profits unless their account is at least $5,000 to $10,000.
4. Other brokers may accept small accounts but, with so many details to take care of, they do not have the time to educate, inform and advise those individuals who hold small accounts.

Fortunately, there is a way to solve those problems. The answer is to form a Commodity Trading Club with a few friends, relatives or business associates. The advantages are:

1. As a group, you can open an account with a larger amount of money. This enables you to trade in commodities and benefit in more ways than you could, individually, on your own.
2. As a group, you can trade in two or more "special situations" when they occur. And you will always have some surplus capital above the margin you need for those trades.
3. As a member of a Commodity Trading Club, you can get together with other investment-minded men and women and make those social meetings pay off.
4. You can discuss investments and ways to make more money when you get together for coffee, at a party or on the phone.

5. You can then use the words, "How much money did we make today?" Most people prefer to use the word WE in this case because it gives them more confidence and a reference point to start a conversation.)

6. With the book, *"How To Build A Fortune In Commodities"* in your hands, you will have a competent reference to help you learn more from discussions with others in your group.

7. After you gain more understanding and know-how, you may decide to increase the size of your share in the Club. Or, if you have enough capital to spare, you may want to use some of that extra money and trade on your own. In this way, you can benefit from the ideas and recommendations given in the weekly "Advisory Letter" that goes to your broker and all of the members of your Club.

As you can see, a Commodity Trading Club is a practical solution to the problem of how the average small investor can trade in commodities and have the same advantages, percentagewise, as the larger traders who have $10,000 or more of capital.

15

ADVISORY SERVICES

Most commodity traders find that it is risky to trade when they base their decision only upon their own thinking. They soon learn that it is helpful to consider the advice of some recognized professional service.

It would seem reasonable to believe that, in an effort to make money for their customers and help them increase their capital, brokerage houses would do their utmost to give their customers nothing but good advice. Surveys, however, show that traders who willingly follow the advice given by brokers in the majority of brokerage firms have been less than profitable to most traders.

Two problems, therefore, face all traders in commodities. One is—the time, effort and the know-how necessary to select "special situations". The other is—the actual selection of those "special situations".

Fortunately, there is a way you can overcome this problem. The first can be solved by the specialists who compile and produce "Chart Services". These services help you save a great deal of time and effort because they can keep you up-to-date on all of the major commodities. Their service includes daily price charts, weekly charts and monthly charts.

When you receive the charts, you will need to spend some time **analyzing them** because you need to determine from those charts which commodities might offer you the best opportunity for a profit.

The second problem can be solved, somewhat, by the Advisory Services. These are specialists who try to help you select the right commodity to buy or sell—at the right time. And a few advisory services try to help you find "special situations". When those "special situations" are pointed out to you, double-check them by (1) going over the charts from the Chart Services. (2) Make certain that all of the points. explained in Chapter 2 are likely to work out in your favor. Then (3) check the "moving averages". The importance of the "moving averages" is explained in Chapter 11.

Write to several advisory services and chart services. Ask them for the facts and fees concerning their service. Also ask the advisory services for a printed "Performance Record".

If the publishers are proud of their record, they will send it to you. If they are not proud of their record and they are not willing to send you a printed Performance Record for at least six months or more, do not subscribe to that service.

Why risk your money? Wait until their recommendations have a good record of performance.

Remember, however, that no advisory service and no advisor will ever be right 100% of the time. There will be losses. Sometimes as often as 50% of the total number of recommendations. The profits, however, should be large enough to more than offset those losses so you can feel that with that advisory service, there is a possibility you can end up each year with a profit.

After you have gotten information from several Advisory Services, if you don't understand one of them, forget it. The information may be too technical for you. Or it may be so full of "ifs" or "double talk" that it may not help you make a worthwhile decision.

Subscribe to at least two of the services that appeal to you the most. The fees for each service are low considering the tremendous amount of work involved getting out the service and the high cost of compiling, printing and mailing that service.

The most helpful commodity service you can buy is the "Worldview Advisory Service." (See address below page.)

This service is designed for serious traders, brokers and the large commercial interests who like to be "right with the trend".

The 4 day, 9 day and 18 day averages are charted for you on the 20 major commodities — Wheat, Corn, Soybeans, Oats, Soybean Oil, Soybean Meal, Lumber, Plywood, Sugar, Cocoa, Silver, Copper, Platinum, Cotton, Live Cattle, Live Hogs, Iced Broilers, Orange Juice, Pork Bellies, Financial Futures, etc.

You will find this valuable, time-saving service gives you three distinct advantages over any other service.

> 1. The extra large charts you receive are easier to read because they are 2 to 4 times larger than any other "bar charts" currently being made.

> 2. These extra large charts give you more confidence because you will have a clearer, more definite "feel" concerning which way each of the 20 major commodities might move — UP or DOWN. (See Chapter 11 for the importance of the "moving averages".)

> 3. The 9 day and the 18 day averages are computed for you and placed on these large charts so you can see "at a glance" which of the 20 commodities you should buy, hold or sell.

These extra long charts with the moving averages computed for you make it easier to earn a larger amount of money with this service than you can from any other service that is, currently, available.

Commodity Trend Service, Inc.
1224 U. S. Hwy., 1-Cove Plaza
North Palm Beach, Fla. 33408

There will, in fact, be times when the profits you can earn
by using this service may be as large as 100% or more in only
a few weeks. You will find it wise, therefore, to have this
service in front of you so you can earn that larger amount of
money.

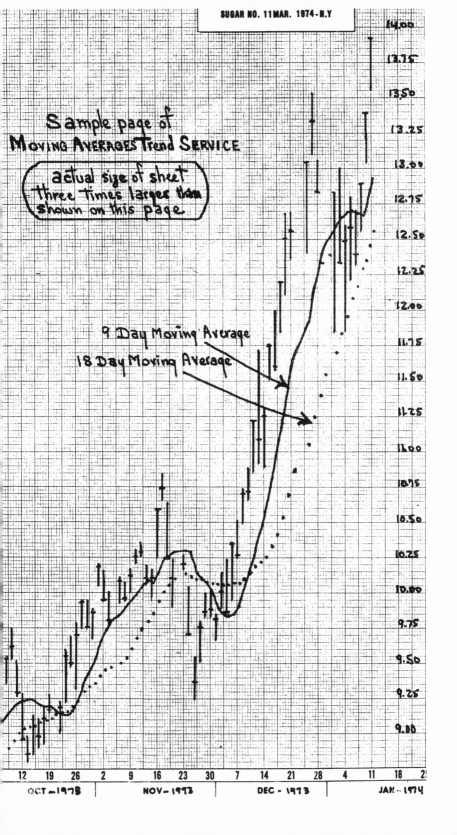

16

SOURCES OF INFORMATION

Success in the futures markets depends on getting reliable information and evaluating that information so you can determine, more easily, which way the market might move based on the fundamentals both present and future.

When you need specific information concerning any commodity, ask your commodity broker. Booklets and pamphlets are prepared by the public relations departments of every one of the major Commodity Exchanges that trade in that commodity. They are free to those traders who are interested. The information and statistics in these brochures can help you know more about that commodity.

In addition, the following reports will give you statistics and information that can help you estimate production and potential supply and demand. None of the reports will give you specific trading advice. It is up to you, therefore, to determine which way the market might move.

*   *   *

The Annual Report (Chicago Board of Trade) lists the daily high, low and closing prices during the year for each month traded. Also gives such statistical data as the carry-over, cash prices, the crop in the United States, world-wide exports and the country where it is shipped, wheat in store in Chicago, loan rates, parity prices, receipts and shipments at Chicago, stocks in all positions and the visible supply.

U.S.D.A. Crop Production Report (released on the 10th of each month) includes the *prospective plantings report* (released March 15th) and the *Annual Summary* issued around December 20th. These reports are widely quoted in the news as the authority in the grain trade.

The Fats and Oils Situation Reports published five times a year by the U.S.D.A. in January, April, June, September and November. Gives professional comments on general economic conditions affecting the soybean yield, crushing and exports, processor's margins, etc. Provides summaries on most of the important statistical data about soybeans, soybean oil and other competing fats and oils.

Wheat Situation Report issued four times each year by the U.S.D.A. in March, May, August and November. It consists of data and articles that discuss the wheat fundamentals, recent developments, government programs current outlook, the world wheat situation and the prospect for the coming year.

The Hogs and Pigs Report is issued four times each year by the U.S.D.A. The information in these reports is only an estimate taken by statements given by the farmers. Market conditions and prices may cause those farmers to change their minds so you need to keep flexible. Use these reports to compare with the figures given a year earlier. When you understand them, you can estimate the potential production of hogs six months ahead.

Quarterly Pig Crop Reports. These reports are important because they indicate changes in the hog cycle. A sharp increase in the farrowings may cause farmers to cut back their herds because lower prices and reduced profits may be ahead. If the quarterly report indicates that hog slaughter in 4 to 6 months will be 6% more than a year earlier, it means that prices could be 12% to 15% lower than a year earlier.

U.S.D.A. Cotton Production Report. This comes out around May 8th. Other reports are issued around the 8th of each month from July through December.

Broiler Report. This report gives the total number of egg sets and placements. Obtain this report from—Statistical Reporting Service, 203 No. Governor St., Richmond, Va. 23219.

Commitments of Traders in Commodity Futures. This report is issued by the Commodity Exchange Authority in Chicago. It gives you the open interest of holders of both the long and the short positions in this way:

> Large traders:
> Speculative
> Long or short only
> Long and short (spreading)
> Hedging
> Small traders
> Speculative and hedging

After this report is gone over and analyzed, many traders prefer a position in line with the positions held by the large traders. If the large traders are mostly long, prices may soon move up. If they are mostly short, prices may soon move lower.

The U.S.D.A. address is United States Department of Agriculture, Washington, D.C. 20250

*   *   *

17

HOW TO SELECT A BROKER

Every year, the number of people who trade in commodities has increased. Most of the larger brokerage houses that deal in stocks and bonds now trade in commodities because so many of their customers want to trade in these faster-moving markets.

One reason why so many speculators like to trade in commodities is the ease with which it can be done. Some registered brokers, however, do not like to handle commodity trades because their minds are not agile enough to handle the many rapid trades each day. They prefer, instead, to specialize in the slower-moving stocks or mutual funds.

In addition to the larger brokerage houses, there are a growing number of firms that have decided to specialize in commodities. These brokerage houses believe that, as specialists, they can offer better service and their efforts seem more professional than most of their competitors in the larger stock and commodity firms.

Occasionally, these specialists in commodities do well. At other times, they do not. So, in the final analysis, you will need to be as professional as possible yourself. You will then be willing to trade on their judgment only after you have double-checked the rules and plans you have learned in this book.

After you select the brokerage firm, you should then select a broker you like. In the majority of cases, the firm you select will assign a broker to you. He may or may not be the best one for you personally. If you feel that is true, get acquainted with one or two others or ask the manager of the office to select another broker.

In addition to his knowledge and ability to render good service, your broker needs good judgment. But the broker, of course, is not the answer to successful trading. And, occasionally, during the year, his judgment may not be as good as at other times during the year. At such times, you may need to rely more heavily on your own judgment, plus the Rules given in Chapter 10. And the ideas given in the book—"The Professional Trading System" will also help you earn larger profits from commodities.

There are two ways to select a broker. One is to visit the office of the large stock brokerage firms. If they have a commodity department, ask to see one of the older, more experienced men. The other is to seek out a brokerage firm that specializes only in commodities and never deals in stocks. Such firms try to be specialists and they are, sometimes, quite knowledgeable. Experience has proven, however, that no broker in commodities can help you select the right commodity at the right time and help you earn a profit on every trade. There will be times when you will have to take losses.

There are several reasons for that fact:

1. The broker is too close to the market. The news he receives each day may cause him to judge the market according to that news. (You will find in Chapter 2 why that viewpoint is not always helpful to successful trading.)

2. Many of his customers may be trading in a certain commodity at a certain price level. He may then hope that your trade will help to move that market in the direction he and those customers would like it to move. But the number of contracts you, as a single individual, may buy or sell will affect the market trend very little—if any. Only concentrated buying or selling can cause a market to move significantly. The effort of one broker in one office has very little effect.

3. The desires of the customers in each brokerage office may vary. Some may want to trade only in grains, some in meats, some in cotton, some in cocoa, sugar, silver, lumber, etc. And each customer asks the broker for his opinion and advice. This tends to cause the broker to be confused. He soon realizes he cannot be knowledgeable concerning so many commodities. And he finds it difficult to give you an honest and dependable opinion.

4. The majority of brokers are too commission-conscious. Too often they try to encourage their customers to trade even though no good trading opportunity is indicated. If you are one of those customers so encouraged, you may wind up with a loss instead of a profit. If you consult an Advisory Service before you trade, it may prove helpful to you.

Some people make the mistake of expecting too much from a broker. They try to pressure him and sort of insist he do a better job for them. But no active broker is paid to be an analyst, statistician or advisor. His primary job is to place orders to buy or sell. He is usually too busy or too close to the market to offer you profitable trading advice—except on occasions when the trend—up or down—is obvious and clear.

A broker, of course, out of courtesy and a desire to help, will give you an opinion and a judgment but, if he is busy, do not expect him to say, "I have spent the past few hours or days analyzing this situation."

Instead of long study and research, most brokers give you snap judgments—whatever "they feel" may happen in the market. Or they may give you advice which is fundamentally right, but if they are right at the wrong time, the market can go against you for several days.

WHAT TO LOOK FOR

When you look for a commodity broker, ask yourself these questions:

1. How much experience has the firm had in commodities?

2. What information and news can the firm supply?

3. Do they subscribe to one or more advisory services or do they rely solely on information supplied by their own firm?

4. Do they have fast wire service direct to each major exchange?

5. Do they show a willingness to help you learn more about commodities? If they take the attitude, "Listen to me, I know what to do", forget them. Nobody and no brokerage firm knows exactly what to do. Commodity trading is an art—not a cut and dried routine.

It is important to remember that most good brokers have a limited amount of time during each day. They are too busy.

They must continually answer the phone, read papers and news, talk to new customers and write up orders. (Some of those orders will be to buy and others will be to sell the same commodity at almost the same price.) Brokers, therefore, do not have the time to relax, select special situations and carefully analyze those situations to find out where the best opportunities lie.

Some brokers, however, can help you more than others. Only time and talking with brokers in various offices can help you find one you like.

HOW TO OPEN AN ACCOUNT

First, look in the "yellow pages" of the telephone directory in the city nearest you. Under the heading of Investment Securities or Brokers-Commodities or Commodity Brokers, you will find one or more brokerage firms.

Once you choose a brokerage firm, it is easy to open an account. Various papers need to be signed. The first is the customer's margin agreement. This is to make certain you agree to trade in a business-like way and be responsible for any losses you may have.

The other form is the authority to transfer funds. This is necessary because when you trade in regulated commodities after trading in non-regulated commodities, your broker must have the right to transfer those funds as they are needed.

You may then place your orders personally in the broker's office or by telephone. Most orders, however, are placed by telephone. After the order has been placed, the broker will mail you a confirmation of the trade after the close of business on the day the trade was made. This confirmation will tell you the size of your position. When you close out your position, the confirmation will then include the price, the amount of profit or loss and the total commission paid.

Commodities may also be traded by partnerships, trading clubs and corporations. In partnerships and trading clubs, all the partners must agree to allow the account to be opened and must designate which partner or partners can act for the partnership. Corporations must state in their charter, or by a special amendment, that commodity trading will be allowed as part of their corporate business. The broker will also require a special form for Corporations to be filled out before he can accept orders to trade for that Corporation.

The policy of the brokerage firm may vary. Some firms require a minimum deposit of $1,000. Others may require as much as $5,000. Most brokers believe it is difficult to earn much money with any deposit less than those amounts. They say, "$5,000 of risk capital will give you a reasonable chance to earn a large amount per year. $10,000 as a minimum would be preferable."

If you have only a limited amount of capital, the only solution to this problem is to form a Commodity Trading Club with friends, relatives or business associates so that you will have a larger amount of capital to work with. (See Chapter 14, *Why Not Start A Commodity Trading Club?*)

One large brokerage firm says, "If losing money in your account would alter your life style, you should not be a commodity speculator. We only want customers in our firm with money they can afford to lose. We will do everything we can to help them win because, then, our business will grow."

If you want your account to be managed by someone other than yourself, the broker will require a limited power of attorney or trading authority. This will allow the broker to take orders from that person in your name.

A power of attorney will allow the account manager to withdraw money as well as trade your account. Some brokers do business in managed accounts. These are subject to minimum capital requirements larger than the amount required from accounts which are not managed by brokers.

Be very cautious before you sign an authority for someone else to trade your account. And that is particularly true if the account manager may be interested, primarily, in the amount of commissions he may earn.

TYPES OF ORDERS

You may buy or sell a commodity in five different ways:

1. At a specified price—if it is reached.

2. At the market. This means the broker must execute your order promptly at the best price possible, but not at a fixed price. A limit may be placed on such a "market order". This requires that the broker must not pay more than that limit price in the case of a buy order nor sell for less than that limit in the case of a sell order. Such an order assures you that you will get at least the price you want if the order is

executed, but there is also the possibility, when you place a limit on a trade, that you may not get your order filled if it is not possible for the broker on the floor of the exchange to fill the order at that specified limit.

3. Stop loss orders. A "buy on stop" order informs your broker that you want to buy "at the market" when a commodity rises to the price you specify. A "sell on stop" order informs your broker that you want to sell "at the market" when a commodity declines to the price you specify. Stop orders may be given to a broker for these three reasons:

1. To limit a loss if the market goes against you.

2. To protect a profit. If the market is going your way, you keep moving your stop higher in a bull market and lower in a bear market so that, if the market should ever turn around and start to move in the opposite direction, you will be out of the market with a profit.

3. To enter a new position. There will be times when you are not certain whether a market will break out in the direction you want it to go—up or down—but you feel that if it should break out you want to be sure to buy or sell at that point so you can get in on the move. Such an order in a bull trend is given—"buy on stop at (you name the price) or, in a bear trend,—"sell on stop at".

4. A "market if touched order" (a broker will write it up as M. I. T.) is executed "at the market" when the price reaches a certain specified level. This type of order is used by many chart traders. When they believe that a particular move has reached the point where they feel a sale is indicated, they will place an order which reads "sell at (the price) market if touched". This means that if they want to get out of a long position or want to sell short at that point, as soon as the price is reached, they will accept any price immediately thereafter. In some cases, the next price might be a bit higher. At other times, it might be a bit lower. In either case, they have made a sale at a price level that seems reasonable to them. If they are short, the order will read, "Buy at (price) market if touched". And again, that price might be a bit lower or a little higher.

5. Scale orders. These are used when you want to establish new positions or liquidate old positions as the market moves up or down. When you are long and you desire to sell out

tell your broker to sell one contract at one price, another at a slightly lower price, and so on until all of your contracts have been sold. And, if you are short, you tell your broker to buy one contract at one price, another at a slightly lower price and so on until all of your contracts have been bought.

The only problem with scale orders is—the market must continue to move in your favor. If it does not, you cannot sell your contracts at higher prices. The market might, instead, turn around and move down before those contracts have been closed out. In such a case, you should have "stop loss orders" to protect yourself as outlined in point 3 above.

BUYING POWER OR EXCESS MARGIN

Whenever you have made a trade and the market moves in your favor, you will have a profit and the further the market moves in your favor, the larger that profit will be. If you do not take out your profit, you will have an excess of capital in your account. This excess gives you additional trading power. With that excess, you can buy more of that same commodity (without putting up additional money) or you can buy some other commodity. (Your broker will explain how this is done.) You should, however, make certain you raise your stops to protect your profit so that, if the market turns around, you will still have some profit and enough capital to plan another trade.

TIPS FROM A PROFESSIONAL TRADER

To succeed at anything, you must understand it. You must have some source of accurate, reliable advice and information. If your broker cannot supply it, you must look to an advisory service (see Chapter 15) to supply you with the information, ideas and trading advice you need.

* * *

Try to be conservative. The more of a follower you are— the greater your possibilities for success. Aggressiveness and taking a chance will cost you more money than you can win.

Experienced traders wait. They look for a good buy—a "special situation." Inexperienced traders, however, jump in when they hear the news is bullish. They believe they should join the crowd and buy. They "see" the opportunity "too late." Usually they want to buy when the market has already reached a top.

There is a difference between going into the market because prices "are up" and because prices "should go up". In fact, that is the big difference between profits and losses. A good trader will try to buy either at the bottom or near the bottom—when few people are interested—or at least no later than the half-way point.

* * *

Once you make up your mind and determine which commodity you want to trade—act. Delays and procrastination can let some good opportunities slip by. And, no matter what happens, persevere. Don't ever become displeased with commodities and quit. The world is full of quitters. They make it easy for the ambitious ones to succeed. Eventually, you will learn all you need to know about trading in commodities. Then you will have a better feel for the various markets. This book, for example, can be a great help.

Many traders have lost all they had in the market. They learned, however, what not to do. They came back and regained it. In this way, they proved it doesn't take much money to succeed, but it does take a great deal of determination and willingness to learn. And, those who can learn, eventually *build a fortune in commodities*—or, at least, a consistent income.

*   *   *

Money is easier to make than to keep. It is wise, therefore, to continually take money out of the market. As your profits increase, do not try to pyramid those profits hoping to "get rich in a hurry".

Put at least one-half of your profits into some form of good security, high grade bonds, good real estate, or pay off any debts you may have.

When you use your profits to increase the number of contracts you hold. you will eventually lose most or all of your money. The larger number of positions will increase your risk. When the market turns against you—and it usually does just at the time when you become more confident—your losses will increase and your equity can then be wiped out in a hurry.

What you had gained in 6 to 8 weeks may then be lost in 3 to 5 days.

*   *   *

Everyone makes mistakes. That, in itself is not a weakness. The weakness comes when you fail to learn from the mistakes you make.

*   *   *

In addition to courage **and know-how,** you must be persistent. If you want to succeed, on a long-term basis, you must keep trying and never give-up. President Calvin **Coolidge understood the value of persistence. He stated it in this way.**

> Nothing in the world can take the place of persistence. Talent will not because there is nothing more common than unsuccessful men with talent. Genius will not. In fact, unrewarded genius is almost a proverb. Education will not. That is why the world is full of educated derelicts. Persistence and determination, alone, are omnipotent.

*   *   *

You cannot make a profit on every trade. But you can be careful in your selection and, thereby, keep your losses small. Professional traders, for example, know their judgment is not perfect because the action of the market is not perfect. And the patterns the market creates are caused by the actions of imperfect people. They hope, therefore, to lose on no more than 40% of their trades, to win on 50% and break even on 10%. This means that the selections you make should earn a profit of 60% or more when you are right. Those profits will then offset the losses you take when you are wrong.

*   *   *

As a general rule, whatever profit you may want to earn in stocks, you may earn in 1/10th time when you trade in commodities. For example, if you believe you can double your money in ten years in stocks, you can double your money in one year or less in commodities. Whatever you believe you can earn in 5 years in stocks, you may earn the same amount in six months in commodities.

*   *   *

From a practical point of view, there is no such thing as "luck" in the market. Capital is less of an asset than knowledge. A good trader will need little capital to regain whatever capital he may lose, but capital without knowledge can soon be lost. Then—all you have is experience. Hopefully, that experience will lead to knowledge or, at least, a desire for knowledge.

*   *   *

There will be many times every year when you will find it wise to stay out of the market. Continuous trading—always in the market—is a disease. There must be times when you should do nothing. Take a rest period. Then, after a week or so, look for a "special situation" in one or more commodities. Study that special situation. Should you buy or sell short? See if the potential profit may be at least three times larger (60%) against the 20% potential loss you may have to take. If the ratio does indicate three to one in your favor —and you have had a rest away from the market—enter an order to buy or sell—according to that situation.

As an example, take the professional in sports. He will train hard, learn what to do and what not to do, then get ready for that one big opportunity for which he is paid. When that bout or game is over—and he has earned his money—he relaxes. He forgets all about that activity for awhile until the time comes to prepare for another opportunity to win. This helps to keep him fresh and professional rather than stale and ineffective from overwork or too much activity.

*   *   *

Whether you make money or lose will depend on how you interpret the movement of a market. Everyone makes mistakes now and then. If your interpretation is wrong, how quickly will you admit it, reverse your position and stop your losses? To stick with your mistakes just because you want to prove "I said so" is like fighting windmills. A Don-Quixote-like attitude will never make you a good trader.

*   *   *

Good luck occurs quite often in commodity trading. Attractive opportunities show up sometimes once or twice each month. Good traders know how to gain the maximum amount of profit. They let the big move develop, then they take a large amount of profit from that move rather than try to take small profits many times along the way. In fact, it will really amaze you to learn how much more profitable it is to trade only once or twice each month rather than try to trade every day or every week.

*   *   *

Your goal should be approximately 360% per year—30% per month. If you trade on a conservative basis, 360% per year means that you need a profit of only $1\frac{1}{2}\mathcal{c}$ on Pork Bellies—six times per year. Or $2\mathcal{c}$—four times per year. In Wheat, Corn or Soybeans, it means you should try to secure a profit of only $8\mathcal{c}$ per bushel—six times per year. Or $10\mathcal{c}$ per bushel—four times per year. In Cotton, it means you need to take a profit of $2\mathcal{c}$—4 times each year. Or $3\frac{1}{4}\mathcal{c}$—twice each year.

Obviously, to obtain such fortunate results, you must look for and trade only in "special situations". After you have selected a special situation, self-discipline is needed. Tell yourself to act—then do it. Then be patient. If your position is right, hold on until you have earned the profit you would like to have on that move.

If you are wrong, get out. Many new opportunities will come along—in the future—that will help you overcome all of your losses. If you take advantage of that new opportunity, you will be more certain of ending each year with a profit.

MOST TRADERS MAKE MISTAKES

Fortunately—for you—most traders make mistakes. And the more mistakes they make, the easier it is for you, as a serious, professional trader, to make a profit. There are six mistakes most amateurs will make:

1. They get so interested in a certain commodity they fail to see the big profits coming from "special situations" in other commodities.

2. They fall in love with their charts until they begin to believe the charts they keep will tell them exactly what to do. Then, just as they become 100% certain, prices move in the opposite direction and they cannot understand why their charts misled them. (One reason is— they forgot to analyze the fundamentals and try to determine what those fundamentals might be — in the future.)

3. They get too greedy. They want to sell at the top or buy at the bottom. In an effort to get the maximum amount of profit, they lose much of that profit because they waited too long. The biggest and fastest profits are made from the move—in the middle—between the top and the bottom. (It is best to take that big profit then look for another "special situation".)

4. They get tied up in "trading markets" in which prices move up and down over a comparatively narrow, indecisive price range. Sometimes, they try to outguess such a market. They buy and "hope" the market will move higher. A few days later, prices turn around and decline to a lower level. "News" will then be given out that may induce them to sell in hopes of lower prices. Then, once again, the market turns around and goes up. They are "whipsawed" and lose in both cases. (That is why it is so important to stand aside sometimes and look for "special situations".)

5. They are lazy. They do not like to spend the time necessary on details such as compiling the "moving averages," analyzing the charts, checking the fundamentals and trying to put the three together in an effort to make a wise decision.

6. They are unwilling to spend the money necessary to have the right tools that help lead to success. Charts, books, paper market reports, "moving averages" and research are needed. Careless traders try to save a few hundred dollars each year on such items.

They fail to realize that commodity trading is a business and every business has necessary expenses. Some businesses have more expense than others. But commodity trading is one business that can be conducted at a comparatively low expense.

If, for example, you own a business in which you have invested $20,000 and hope to earn a net profit of 10% ($2,000 per month), you might have to spend $5,000 or more every month ($60,000 per year) for employees, rent, telephone, advertising, insurance, lights, water, etc. When you trade in commodities, however, you can earn that same $2,000 per month with an investment of less than $10,000. Your total expense should be 5%. That is much less than the $60,000 of expense required each year to operate the average small business mentioned above.

In fact, you may find that only $100 per month ($1,200 per year) should give you all the tools and help you need — charts, books, reports, research, advisory services etc.

Very few traders who compete with you in commodities will ever spend that $100 per month ($1,200 per year). They try to cut corners and save. I have seen many of them use scraps of paper to keep charts or record the quotations. Yet they hope that, with such inefficient tools, they can earn as much money, percentagewise, as the professionals.

* * *

Good trading improves with practice, a keen sense of timing and an intelligent application of the rules and principles contained in Chapter 10.

* * *

FUNDAMENTALS ARE IMPORTANT

Above all, remember that the fundamentals are important. Accurate analysis of the market requires that the fundamentals should be followed closely and revisions must be made as new fundamentals become available.

My axiom is—when the fundamentals change, you must change. You cannot fight against the trend in the market that the change in those fundamentals will bring.

The price of all commodities will always move up or down to justify the news at some time—in the future. If the news concerning a commodity has been bad for several weeks, the market will tend to make a bottom for a move upwards towards higher prices. Why? Because, in a few more weeks or months, the news will be better and prices will then rise to justify that better news.

If the news for several weeks has been very good, prices will tend to move down because conditions will soon change. Producers, processors and suppliers will find ways to increase the supply or they will decide to buy less of that commodity at such a high price. The supply will then tend to increase so the commercial interests can buy what they need at lower prices. The news will then become less bullish and prices will move down to justify the more bearish news that will come sometime — in the future.

In other words, the price of all commodities will move up or down toward a level that makes "the news" come true so that, when the good news eventually comes, the price will justify that news. At that point, professional traders will say, "the news has been discounted in the market."

As a market dealing in "futures", that is the way it should be. If that news has been discounted by the market a few days or even a few weeks in advance of the day the news is released, it will have little impact on the market. Prices may even turn around and move in the opposite direction because sometime—in the future—the news will be better. (See charts on page 38 in Chapter 2.)

Every commodity has three characteristics. First, the expiring month and the cash price tend to come together as the future contract goes off the board. Second, if the total supply is normal or larger than normal, each of the distant future months will sell at a higher price than the month that precedes it. Third, if there is a shortage of supply, the near months will sell at a higher price than each of the more distant months.

If certain commodities are inclined to move very little or stay in a "trading range", look for other commodities that offer a better potential for profit. There are three factors to look for:

1. Does the commodity look like it might be a "special situation?"
2. Is the total volume and open-interest increasing? (This is necessary as prices move higher in a bull market or move lower in a bear market).
3. Is it possible that the fundamentals, in a few more weeks, will justify a higher price for a good bull move— or—a lower price for a good bear move?

* * *

When there is a large volume of trading in a commodity with little improvement in price, it is an indication that "distribution" is being done by those "in the know" who bought that commodity at much lower levels. They are selling to less informed people who prefer to buy when the news is good. As soon as no more buyers are found who are willing to buy at those high prices, the volume of sales each day will tend to fall off. The market is then due for a reversal.

As the buying dries up, selling in the form of profit-taking by longs and "short sales" by professional short-sellers plus hedge sales by the commercial interests will cause the market to decline.

If the volume and the price both increase at high levels, it is a good sign that prices may soon move higher. If the volume decreases as prices go down, the decline will not last long and a rally will soon occur.

In either case, be patient, the market does not change course overnight. It usually takes several days to several weeks for a market to complete a top or form a bottom. If you are impatient and buy or sell too soon, you may enter the market prematurely. In other words, you could be "right at the wrong time."

If prices do not turn around and move in your favor that same day, you may suffer a loss as prices continue to move in their recent direction.

The "moving averages" will give you a better indication of this.

If a rally or an upmove develops because "shorts" have

covered and you notice a decrease in the open-interest, the technical condition of the market becomes weak. The "shorts" must always be regarded as a potential buying force. If they have already bought (covered their shorts), then the potential buying force is less than it was at lower levels. The rally, therefore, will soon die.

BEFORE YOU TRADE—ESTIMATE YOUR RISK

Before you enter a trade—even if you believe it is a special situation—you must know whether the profit you wish to make is at least three times more than the risk you are willing to take. This means you should try to earn a minimum potential profit of 60% per trade against a maximum loss of 20% or less.

Efforts to day trade, "scalp the market" or attempt to earn small profits are not wise. Those who trade in that manner earn very little money and, eventually, most of them lose. The small profits are not worth the great amount of time and effort necessary to trade so often. It is wiser to relax, take it easy and trade only once or twice each month so you can be more certain of earning 360% or more per year.

*   *   *

The greatest mistake you can make in life is to never take a chance. In fact, those who fail to take a chance find that life becomes dull. There is no excitement to give them a thrill or a lift. They find they exist, but they do not live.

Most individuals who trade in anything, including commodities, will make mistakes and lose money several times before they achieve success. Those who are wise learn that great men are never afraid to make a mistake. They accept their losses without spending too much time on regret. Then they try to do better the next time. And, most important, they keep trying when others with less courage advise them to "quit".

WHAT CAUSES PRICES TO CHANGE

There are several conditions that cause prices to change:

1. At the bottom, speculators who are short will buy back those shorts. Commercial interests who placed "selling hedges" (see Chapter 3) several months earlier will buy back those selling hedges. Other speculators and commercial interests will buy and take a long position. They believe a bottom has been made or at least, a rally is due.

2. Commercial interests who have sold a commodity for future delivery will place a "buying hedge" in the futures market to make certain they will have that amount of the commodity available when it comes time to make that future delivery.

3. As prices gain support, other commercial interests believe prices may not move lower so, in order to meet current needs and production requirements, they will buy—usually "at the market".

4. Traders who sense the market has turned from bearish to bullish now enter the market and add their "buy orders" to those of the commercial interests. Prices then will rise because there are more orders to buy than to sell.

5. An increase in the production of any commodity can create a surplus. That surplus can cause prices to fall. The larger the surplus, the larger that decline in price may be. And, conversely, when there is a decrease in production, a shortage may occur. This can help to create an increase in the price of the futures.

*   *   *

The reason prices do not move up in a straight line without any decline is—every day some of the traders who are long decide to sell and take profits, a few commercial interests sell their "buying hedges" because they filled their contracts in the cash market and a few traders will "sell short" hoping they may make a profit on a possible decline.

DO NOT TRADE IN SPREADS

Some traders try to make a profit by buying one future month and selling another. This is called a "spread". It is the sale of one commodity contract against the purchase of another. The profit or loss comes from a change in their relationship.

Trading in spreads should never be undertaken by anyone who is not a skilled trader. In fact, I personally do not recommend them. If you can judge the general trend of the market —up or down—why be involved in a situation where one side of the spread is going to move against you?

The only exception to that is—a temporary hedge. Assume you are long in a commodity and the price moves up for several days. You now have a nice profit. You feel there may be a reaction but you do not want to lose your basic position so you sell one or more contracts short (depending on how many contracts you are long). You tell your broker to "sell at the market"—don't try to get a specific price in this case.

What happens now? If prices continue to move higher, you will continue to make a profit on your longs, but you will lose on the contracts you sold short. This type of spread will, obviously, earn you more money than the spread where you sell short at the bottom of the move at the same time you go long or buy at the top of the market at the same time you sell another month "short".

In brief, "spreads" are only good for brokers who are (1) uncertain which way the market will move or (2) they want you to trade both sides of the market so they can double their commissions.

STAY OUT OF TRADING MARKETS

Trading markets should be left alone. The many small moves up and down are frustrating. You enter the market and believe it should move in your favor, but it doesn't. It turns around and moves against you. News and rumors are put out to convince traders they should get out of their position and trade in the opposite direction. If you do so, prices may soon turn around and, once again, go against the trend you want. Each time you are "whipsawed", you will lose money as you try to make a profit on each turn.

If you do not trade and reverse your position each time the market turns around and, instead, you ride the movement of prices up and down, you will find that, after several weeks or months, you are still in about the same place as the day you started. Like riding an elevator, you have seen much activity take place, but you have actually made no progress.

You may lose no money or very little money "riding the elevator" in that way, but you can definitely lose time. And time is valuable—especially when you realize that time can never be regained.

Triangles, flags, pennants and areas of distribution and accumulation are all trading markets. They are, generally, confusing. If you give those markets time to make up their minds which way they want to go, you can trade with less risk as you wait and go with the market as prices "break out" from those formations. Whatever profits you earn will usually be too small to be worth the time, effort and frustration of trading in that market.

Let others waste their time and money in trading markets. You are now much wiser. You prefer instead, to look for and trade in "special situations". And, furthermore, a trading market will seldom, if ever, allow you to earn 60% or more profit on every trade—and that is the minimum profit you should look for in "special situations."

Brokers, who are short-sighted, may not favor that trading plan. In their desire to earn commissions, they may prefer that you trade more often. But all brokers know from experience that 90% of the traders who try to "play the market" every day will lose money. It seems to me that brokers will profit more on a long-term basis, if they encourage their customers to make money every month and increase the size of their account by 30% or more, as pointed out in this book, than try to find new customers to replace the 90% short-term traders who lose money.

*   *   *

In the September, 1972 issue, COMMODITIES magazine, printed an article called, *"Probing the Mind of the Professional Trader"*. Some of the comments made by several experienced professionals are as follows:

"I classify myself as 85% a fundamentalist who never ignores a spontaneous urge. If I'm long and feel the market is tired or not acting well, I don't hesitate to get out and take another look."

"If you get an intuitive feeling and you act on it, then you can always get back in. If you reduce your position or even it up, you can look at things a little more objectively. It's very easy to fall in love with a position. This is the danger facing any trader, whether a chartist, computerist or what have you—that is, failing to recognize the signals the market is giving you."

"The worst time to make a trade is when the news is a month after the actual fact. That just tells you why the market was doing what it did. It doesn't tell you what it is going to do."

"When bullish news comes out and the market does not respond to it, it may be a danger signal that the news has already been discounted."

"A computer is a mechanical system, but I don't think mechanical systems of trading are effective. Computers are only as good as the individuals that advise the programs. And they are not nearly as much fun as charts."

"You have to observe the experts. And the experts in our business are the commercials. When the market rallies sharply, they have always got a little to sell and, when it breaks sharply, they always have a little to buy."

"A trader who has taken a recent loss must be careful not to let it overpower his thinking."

"You have to recognize the obvious—the higher the price goes, the closer it is to the top of the market. And the lower it goes, the closer it is to the bottom."

"A good speculator should review his losing trades. I review my purchases and sales every day. I wait a month, then I go back and study what I did and why I did it. The fun for me is being right."

"A trader or speculator who has sustained a loss must be on guard that the unpleasantness of the loss does not deter him from entering into what may be a profitable trade at a later date."

"Generally, I keep to myself. If I talk too much, I'm not thinking."

"A bullish indicator in July Corn came on June 27 and 28. Open interest had dropped sharply after a long, steady decline. This suggested that the last tired longs had liquidated their positions. It seemed advisable then to buy December Corn."

"When you take into account the major and minor trends of the market, support and resistance patterns, volume, open-interest, and other considerations, then you weigh them. You get probability factors. If you find a standoff in these factors, you are indecisive, you think the market can go either up or down. Then, as the probability factors shift to 60/40, 70/30, 80/20, 90/10—that is when you place your orders."

"I continue to check the latest news and opinions and observe the market action all day long. I adjust my "game plan" according to that news—or, perhaps, I will discard it completely if it doesn't seem to be working."

"Even when an opinion is silly, if it's held by enough people, it will affect the market."

"The experienced trader sits back and watches the orders coming in. After being patient, you start selling carefully when the market stops making new highs. Now you know that what you believed all along has been confirmed. But people who have been buying tend not to believe the news. Therefore, they don't rush to sell."

"When the big play comes, the professionals know what to do. They keep on selling until they are short thousands of contracts—and they'll keep on selling short until prices make new lows before they cover those shorts."

"There is a momentum that builds up, on both the upside and downside, that makes the market move further than it should."

"Careless trading is a temptation even veteran traders find hard to resist."

*   *   *

Don't plan to sell any commodity short on a long-term basis until that commodity has made at least four up moves of six weeks or more duration and four new highs. In a strong bull market, however, there may be five upmoves and a top on the fifth move. Occasionally, if there should be a great shortage of a commodity, there will be six upmoves and, even more rare, there will be seven up moves. But seven would only occur when there is a combination of great shortage and an unusually large amount of speculators in the market. (The decline from the five, six and seven tops are usually very fast and cause large losses if you fail to get out in time as prices move lower).

*   *   *

In commodities, there is no cut and dried, perfect time to buy or sell. But every commodity tends to reach a seasonal high for a sale and a seasonal low for a purchase approximately the same months each year.

After you know the seasonal high or low for a commodity, you may then consider a trade. But first, there are eight requirements before you make that trade.

1. Study the fundamentals. What are they likely to be—in the future.
2. Look over your charts.
3. Analyze which way the market might go—up or down.
4. Wait for a "special situation" to develop.
5. Try to determine what day prices might move in your favor.
6. **Estimate the potential profit—is it 60% or more?**
7. Make certain your loss can be no more than 20%.

8. Follow the rules in Chapter 10.

*   *   *

The following are approximate times each year when you can make plans to buy or sell. Don't make the mistake of believing that, if you buy at the times suggested, the market will always go up, or if you sell at the times suggested, the market will always go down.

Changes in the supply and demand occur in every commodity. When the supply increases, prices will not move up as much as a year or two earlier and they may start to decline a month or so earlier than usual. In fact, if the supply is abnormally heavy at that time, prices may move down instead of up. And, of course, in years of greater demand, prices may move higher than a year or two earlier, or remain around a high price level if the demand for that commodity continues to be large.

LIVE CATTLE—Trading in Live Cattle futures offers large profits for conservative traders who are able to be patient and take advantage of the big moves that occur so often in cattle. The low margins required—usually less than $1,500 and the high profit for every 1 cent (100 point) move gives such conservative traders an excellent chance to earn a large amount on a small investment. Generally, the Live Cattle market is less volatile than other commodities such as Pork Bellies, Soybeans or Silver. The trends both up and down tend to be longer in duration, which makes Live Cattle an excellent medium for those who like to trade for long-term capital gains six months or longer.

Furthermore, an analysis of the Live Cattle market is easier than many other commodities because the fundamentals of supply and demand are, oftentimes, easier to determine.

Severe winter storms can cause a large number of cattle to die. This means fewer cattle are moved to market. So watch the weather in the Midwest and Mountain areas. Also, when the weather is bad, the cattle will seldom gain weight because they need all the food they can consume just to keep warm.

PORK BELLIES—Two seasonal pressure periods usually occur. One in February. The other in August. The February pressure can come from an increase in marketings and slaughter of pigs born in August and September. The August and

September pressure can come from an increase in marketings and slaughter of pigs born in February through April.

LIVE HOGS—The pig crop tends to follow a four year cycle from under-production to over-production back to under-production. This four year cycle occurs because price fluctuations stimulate demand fluctuations. When price goes up, more hogs are farrowed. This results in an oversupply, pulling down prices. Farrowing rates are cut back, resulting in less supply and higher prices again. This cycle has, for the most part, been complete every four years.

EGGS—Trading in egg futures is risky for the average trader because this is a commodity that is very volatile. The fundamentals are difficult to analyze. Only an alert, agile professional chart trader can make money trading in eggs. Others, less agile or not certain of how to forecast potential moves, should not trade in eggs. Futures prices in eggs may respond to cash prices and prices often change quickly. Many traders can be "wiped out" even though they can see no immediate change in the basic figures for supply and demand.

CORN—After the harvest has been "hedged" during August, September and early October, futures prices tend to move higher. Prices during December are generally higher than those of October and November. Then, during January till March prices usually show a seasonal decline but not to a level as low as prices during the harvest period. This decline is caused, partly, from an accumulation of supplies in Chicago and the close of navigation on the Great Lakes. Prices are also under pressure at this time due to the marketing of high moisture corn which is liable to spoil when the weather warms up in the spring.

A smaller amount of corn marketed during April through June is due to the fact that farmers are spending more time in the fields to produce another crop of corn. In addition, there is usually an increase in demand for livestock feeding during April and May. The Great Lakes open for navigation at this time and, in some years, the shipments of corn through the lakes will reduce the supply of corn in Chicago.

July is considered the most critical growth period for the new crop. There is always a possibility of crop damage at this time. Price levels, therefore, may remain high during July and the early part of August. Later, in August and

September, after livestock feeders have secured the bulk of their needs, the approach of a favorable harvest with an abundance of supplies can cause prices to decline in antici-pation of the new harvest.

WHEAT—Wheat is a grain that can grow well without large amounts of rain. In the spring of the year, two or three days of good rain can often assure a big wheat crop. If rains do not come and the weather is dry for too long a period, the crop may be smaller than normal.

COCOA—There are two fairly reliable times each year when a long position might be taken in Cocoa. One is from around July 15th to August 15th just before the harvest begins. If none of the fundamentals are bearish, a good bull move should occur until around October 10th to 30th. If prices in Novem-ber should move above the highs made in October, it means the total world supply from the main crop is less than needed to supply the demand.

The other time when a long position might be considered in Cocoa is sometime after January 15th up until March 1st. This is after the main.crop has been harvested and you have had an opportunity to evaluate the statistics and the funda-mentals.

As in all commodities, supply and demand can change the dates above, but Cocoa is a commodity that can be traded for large profits by anyone who is a good chart trader and aware of the importance of volume and open-interest.

COPPER—There is a tendency for copper prices to decline until August or early September. Then, if supplies are not burdensome, a bottom may be made for a good move up until sometime late in December or January.

ORANGE JUICE—There is a tendency for Frozen Orange Juice to sell at a low price during June, July and August. During January and February, there is always a possibility prices of Orange Juice futures will rise due to a sudden freeze or a threat of freezing weather. That is why it is risky to sell orange juice "short" until after the end of February.

If the harvest of oranges is late, prices may decline because the later an orange is picked, the more perishable it is and growers usually decide to turn those oranges into frozen concentrate. This can increase the supply of frozen concentrated juice and cause pressure on prices.

POTATOES—Potato prices tend to decline as the harvest begins in September. But, if the crop is comparatively small or not doing well, prices can rise sharply as they did in September, 1972. Contract lows usually occur near January, with prices tending to move up once again until early in May (except in years when the supply is burdensome, then pressure on prices will prevent a bull move from developing).

LUMBER—This commodity is risky and difficult for a trader who does not understand the lumber and building business. Generally speaking, the only way a speculator should trade in lumber is to wait until prices have had a long decline in price. Then, if business conditions in the coming months look favorable, buy lumber at the depressed prices and wait for the long and dramatic rise in price that usually comes. If this plan is followed—and you have the patience—you can often earn a very large percentage of profit.

PLYWOOD—Like lumber, this is a difficult commodity for the average trader. Only an experienced chart reader who is an agile trader should ever enter the plywood market. You can usually earn a large profit trading in Plywood if you will wait, as in the case of lumber, until after a definite, long decline in price. Then buy, hold on, have patience and wait for the profitable rise that seems to occur after each long decline.

YOU MUST HAVE A DEFINITE TRADING PLAN

To be successful, you must have a definite trading plan. It must be practical, easy to use and dependable more times than not. That is why—no matter what your charts say—six points need to be considered before you make a decision to buy or sell.

1. THE FUNDAMENTALS. Will they be bullish or bearish—in the future? If they will be mostly bullish, you can consider going long. Or, if they are likely to be bearish, you can consider going "short"—provided the next five points indicate a move in that direction.

2. THE TREND. Does the trend point up towards a price that—in the future—will justify the bullish fundamentals? If so, you have two points that indicate buy. If the trend points down towards a price that will justify bearish fundamentals —in the future—sell.

3. VOLUME OF SALES. Markets tend to move in the direction of the largest volume of sales. If prices rise and the volume of sales increase, that is a bullish indication. It gives you a third good reason to buy, provided the first two points above are also bullish. If prices decline on large volume and rise on small volume, that is bearish. You should then consider going "short" if the other points in this section are also bearish.

4. OPEN-INTEREST. If the open-interest increases as prices rise, that is a bullish indication. If the open-interest increases as prices decline, that is bearish.

5. SEASONAL FACTORS. All commodities tend to follow a seasonal pattern. Low prices are generally made during certain months and high prices are generally made at certain other months. (Chapters 4, 5, 6 and 7 help you know the seasonal influence. You can also double check by studying the long-term charts given in each of those three chapters.) A note of caution, however. During periods of great shortage or large supply, the seasonal factors are not as dependable because, at those times, prices will stay at high levels for a longer period during shortages, or stay around low levels for a longer period due to the large supply which must be reduced.

6. SUPPLY AND DEMAND. If reports and estimates show there will be a shortage of a commodity—in the near future—you have another reason to buy—if the other five points above also indicate a bullish trend. If those reports indicate a larger supply will soon be coming to market, you have another reason to "sell short."

Make certain that all of the six points above agree on the possible move—up or down. If your charts and the "moving averages" say, "yes", and the six points above say, "yes", then you can buy or sell according to what they indicate— bullish or bearish.